Caring For Older Relatives

About the Author

Mark Albertson has practiced law since 1987. He is a partner in the law firm of Hanis, Irvine, Prothero, PLLC, in Kent, Washington. Mark is licensed in Washington, Oregon and Alaska, and serves clients in all three states. Mark has focused on estate planning and elder law since 1993, and has helped thousands of clients over his career.

Mark is an active member of the National Academy of Elder Law Attorneys, and was a Charter member of the Academy of Special Needs Planners. Mark is Chair of the Advisory Board of the School of Psychology, Family and Community at Seattle Pacific University, and was appointed in 2012 by Washington's Governor Gregoire to the Board of Trustees of Green River Community College. Mark has served on the Board of Directors of the Senior Housing Assistance Group (SHAG) in Seattle, Washington, and has been named by Seattle Magazine 5 years in a row as a "5 Star Money Manager".

Mark writes a regular Elder and Estate Planning Law Blog, which you can subscribe to at **www.markalbertson.com**.

Mark speaks locally and nationally on elder law and estate planning topics, as well as law practice development and conflict management issues. He has had a radio program in Seattle, and is often called upon to serve as a guest in media on the topic of elder issues.

To Write to the Author

If you wish to contact the author or would like more information, please write to:

Mark Albertson
Attorney/Partner
Hanis Irvine Prothero, PLLC
6703 S. 234th St., Suite 300
Kent, WA 98032
253-520-5000
malbertson@hiplawfirm.com

Caring For Older Relatives

Legal, Health, Caregiving and Financial Issues with Older Adults

2013 Edition

Mark Albertson
Attorney at Law

www.markalbertson.com

Jedeye Press
Seattle, Washington

Caring for Older Relatives:
Legal, Health, Caregiving and Financial Issues with Older Adults

2013 Edition

ISBN 978-1-300-44310-0

Published by Jedeye Press, PO Box 541, Seattle, WA 98035

Printed in the United States of America

What a blessed influence the old exert in cherishing feelings of reverence, affection and subordination in families; in warning the young against the temptations and allurements of the world; in detailing the results of experience, in exposing the fallacies of worldly maxims; in rebuking the recklessness of indiscretion and the experiments of enthusiasm; in imparting judicious counsel in church and State and private life; --in short, how much good of every kind is accomplished by the tranquilizing, wise and conservative influences of age.

(Rev. Cortlandt Van Rensselaer Old Age: A Funeral Sermon 1841)

DISCLAIMERS

This information is provided "as is". The author, publishers and marketers of this information disclaim any loss or liability, either directly or indirectly as a consequence of applying the information presented herein, or in regard to the use and application of said information. No guarantee is given, either expressed or implied, in regard to the merchantability, accuracy, or acceptability of the information.

The legal issues presented are for educational purposes only. The law, and particularly the law in the area of elder law, changes with great frequency, and is different not only from state to state, but often, from county to county. Please seek qualified legal advice before undertaking any strategy discussed in this book. The author takes no responsibility for the information in this book, and assumes no attorney-client relationship through this book. Readers should not assume that either.

Further, this information is not presented by a medical practitioner and is for educational and informational purposes only. The content is not intended to be a substitute for professional medical advice, diagnosis, or treatment. Always seek the advice of your physician or other qualified health provider with any questions you may have regarding a medical condition. Never disregard professional medical advice or delay in seeking it because of something you have read.

Since natural and/or dietary supplements are not FDA approved they must be accompanied by a two-part disclaimer on the product label: that the statement has not been evaluated by FDA and that the product is not intended to "diagnose, treat, cure or prevent any disease."

Contents

Preface 1

Caring for Your Older Relatives: When Does it Begin? 3

Financial and Estate Planning Issues 7

Determining Who Takes Responsibility for Aging Parents 17

Who Becomes the Caregiver? 23

Accelerating Care Needs 27

Paying for Long-Term Care 39

Medical Care for Older Adults 65

Nutritional Needs for Older Adults 69

Moving and Your Older Relative 73

Dealing with Depression in Older Adults 77

Safe Driving 81

Elder Safety 85

Understanding Confusion 89

Know the Professionals 95

Taking Care of the Caregiver: Preventing and Identifying Caregiver Stress 113

Conclusion 119

Preface

In 1900, life was very different from today. Most Americans still lived on farms or in multi-generational housing. The average lifespan of an American was about 41 years of age. Families lived together, and it was not uncommon for three generations to live in the same household. Most Americans were not transitory. They were often born and died in the same home. There was a place for everyone in the family. When family members were young, they had chores to do. As they grew older they harvested the crops, took care of the livestock and mended fences. And as they grew old, they were needed to help with the household, raise children, and to take care of the less physical aspects of life. There was a social contract given to family members: You will be taken care of until you die. There were few "nursing homes" and the concept of "assisted living" and "adult family homes" had not even entered our imaginations.

Today, we look at a very different demographic. By 2050, the 65 and older population is projected to be close to 87 million. The 75 and older population is projected to be close to 49 million and the number of people age 85 and older is projected to increase to 7.3 million in 2020. Three generations living in the same state is rare, much less the same household. The social contract does not exist with any regularity today. To have children to rely on is a rare thing, and with the majority of women having careers, it is unrealistic to think that parents will be cared for by their children. Yet in many families across America, our children still try. They work hard every day to balance career, family and parents. Most caregivers receive little praise and support, and very often, even less when they are a family member. Yet they continue to try.

Although many family caregivers are not caring for parents, I will be using "parents" generically throughout this book. Regardless whether they are in-laws, grandparents or others, the principals apply, just the same.

As I put these words on paper, I have spent the last 30 years of my life dedicated to helping people. I received a bachelor's degree in psychology, thinking I was going to be a clinical psychologist. I worked as a social worker in a public mental health center, and, after an experience in which I saw a lawyer stand between a client of mine and a system determined to harm a client, I became a lawyer. I started out life as an estate planning attorney, and still work in that area. I woke up one day, however, looked at my clients and the work I was doing, and realized that I was an *elder law* attorney. Without any conscious decision to become one, and, even before my profession even had a name for the practice focus that has become elder law. Since that time, I have worked with hundreds and hundreds of families who are struggling with the peculiar aspects of aging, and the financial and legal issues that come up simply because of age. I love my profession and the clients I work with.

This guide was inspired by the many family members I have sat with for long hours, struggling to cope with aging relatives. They are my heroes, and I hope this book will provide at least a little guidance. It is very much a summary of many of the issues I help people to struggle with every day, and I hope that writing it down will assist more in their pursuit of a labor of love – taking care of elderly relatives.

Mark Albertson
Attorney at Law
December, 2012

Caring for Your Older Relatives: When does it Begin?

Most parents are heroic people; they bring children into this world, feed them, nurture and love them and accept their idiosyncrasies, no matter what. They sacrifice time and effort to take care of their children and make sure they grow up to be caring and responsible individuals.

Parents are fallible, flawed human beings, but they are also superheroes. They are our superheroes, because they got up every morning, with no formal training, and did their best, no matter what limitations they had, and raised their children. Some did better than others, but most did the very best job they were capable of doing. Yes, they made mistakes. Yes, they were always restrained by the times and by the expectations of their own particular generation, but most of our parents cared deeply for us.

Good, bad or indifferent, parents are a very important part of the lives of their children. They are responsible for helping to mold their children into what they will become in the future, much like potter molds clay. No person could have managed to become what he or she is without the support of their parents, for better or for worse.

But what happens to parents when they have reared their children and their children lead lives of their own? Parents are human beings and they succumb to old age and health problems that come with being old. Who will take care of them when they become frail and can no longer work to care for themselves?

While most parents do not wish to impose a burden of care on their children, most children feel a moral responsibility to take care of their parents when they can no longer fend for themselves. It is not so much paying back their efforts to rear their children, but has more to do with a strange combination of returning the love that they gave their children when they were still helpless babies until the present, when they are already independent beings, and a sense of duty as the "next" generation.

Financial Issues in the Mix

It is a wonderful situation when our parents have a substantial nest-egg for their care, or have had the forethought to purchase a quality long-term care insurance policy so that their financial needs will be provided for as they get older. The ideal situation is for parents to prepare for their retirement by resorting to a good retirement or financial management plan, including purchasing long term care insurance. This way, parents no longer have to completely rely on their children to take care of their financial and other needs when they are already retired.

There are parents who have prepared well for their retirement and have made investments that can already financially support them and the things they like and need as they grow old. Some parents who were wise enough to prepare for the future spend their retirement days traveling and doing things they did not have time to do before.

Often, however, our parents have not planned well, and for a child to bring up the topic to parents can be incredibly awkward. Very often, children don't know if their parents are in need of their support until it is too late to plan. Modern times and the modern way of living have very often lessened family ties. A person who has elderly parents is often unable to live closer to home or to visit their parents regularly to check on them, and generational "issues" can keep parents from willingly sharing critical financial and legal information with their children until there is a crisis, or until a parent is unable to care for themselves.

Health Issues in the Mix

When parents have substantial health problems or are forgetful, then the children are very often placed in the position of having to be the caregiver. If the children cannot regularly be with their parents, then they may need to arrange for quality healthcare and assisted living for them from a distance. This can be a struggle, especially if parents insist they are still strong and can still take care of themselves when the reality is that they are unable to do so.

While nobody I am aware of plans to go into skilled nursing, Americans have become accustomed to being placed in institutions when they become too old to take care of themselves. This idea can be unthinkable in some families. One positive aspect of modern culture is that there are an array of choices of care, including in-home care, respite care, assisted living, adult family homes and continuity of care communities. While there are more choices, very often these choices can be confusing and intimidating.

Although children often know when their parents are in need of closer attention, when they start to notice changes in parents' attitudes and personal hygiene, these changes can often be subtle and gradual, and often go unmentioned until they become undeniable. Parents who usually dress well and are sociable may be at the brink of desperation and loneliness, when they start to become recluses and refuse to be included in family occasions.

Learning to be aware of changes in parents, even if it is as simple as checking the refrigerator of elderly parents to make sure they have enough stock, and they are eating the right kind of food. It is time to worry when their refrigerator show signs of failure to buy groceries and other food for their daily subsistence. This could mean they have forgotten to shop for their groceries or they are taking their mealtimes for granted

Parents who have become accustomed to being independent may find it difficult to adjust to that period when they require care from another adult. This takes a great deal of patience, and it is important to invest time and effort in making sure parents are given the same love and affection they gave in providing for and raising their children. In some cases, parents were not the best providers or caregivers, which can be a psychological barrier on a child. Nevertheless, it is an opportunity to give unconditionally just because they need you so much at this time in their lives.

Financial and Estate Planning Issues

The Importance of Financial and Estate Planning

It is sound advice that every person who has assets should engage in financial planning, to make sure that their earnings and savings are invested properly during and even after the lifetime of the owner. Proper financial planning helps people to live comfortable lives as they age.

Financial planning is the process or method of knowing the total income and assets of a person and then planning to accomplish their goals, with an eye toward living expenses, retirement, long-term care and lifestyle.

Financial planning can help with the preservation, income generation and growth in value of earnings and properties. Financial planning helps people to be aware of their earnings and assets so they can adequately provide for themselves as they grow older.

The Importance of Retirement Planning

Retirement planning is a particularly important part of financial planning. People who are about to retire but who have not prepared for their retirement finances often face insurmountable obstacles to caring for themselves as they grow older. Fortunately, many people who worked from the 1940's until the 1990's have pension plans which can provide a monthly or annual income for retirees. But what about those who do not have a pension plan—how can they survive when they no longer have a regular income?

Some people plan for retirement at a time when they are still strong and are able to make wise financial decisions. Some of these people have invested their money into retirement plans which will enable them to visit places they have never been to and to do things they did not have the time to do when they were still working.

Estate Planning is a Part of Financial Planning

Financial planning, however, is not just for retirement purposes. An important part of financial planning is estate planning. Death is the only thing certain in this life and every person should prepare for such eventuality. If a person has dependents or beneficiaries then he should name them in a will so that when his time comes, everything would be in order. This can be made possible through proper financial planning.

A person should make sure that he has a will to assure property passes to their intended beneficiaries, and to avoid quarreling between his dependents and beneficiaries at the time of his death. Families usually forget blood relations when it comes to finances so it is better to leave something for everyone and to make this legal and documented through a will.

The estate of a person refers to his entire property or assets including cash, pending income, real estate and other properties like appliances, vehicles, and household fixtures.

When a person plans for his estate, he apportions his properties to his beneficiaries. While a will is made during the lifetime of the deceased, it can only be passed on to the beneficiaries after death.

An important component of estate planning is incapacity planning. Most people become incapacitated, if even for a short period of time prior to their deaths. As an attorney who has represented executors in hundreds of estates, I can honestly say that I see more worse things happen when a person becomes incapacitated than I ever do after someone passes away.

A Checklist of Estate Planning Documents Everyone Needs

I've been asked several times recently, "Mark, do you have some sort of simple checklist of legal documents we should recommend for our parents?" I am not sure if the tide has turned, or if I am more aware now that I am in my 50's, but I have quite a few clients who are concerned about their parents' estate planning, not so much from what they will inherit as much as what tools they'll need to properly care for their parents as they age. So, in an effort to come up with a checklist, here's what will likely be just a first draft of many in the future.

Of course, every person, family and estate plan is different. Most checklists fall short when personalized. So, before you take what I am about to say as gospel, consider sitting down with an estate or elder law attorney, and discuss your own unique situation. That being said, here are some basics that should be on most everyone's list:

1. <u>A will that reflects your parents' desires</u>. Although the statistics are dismal for the number of people who actually execute wills, the statistics are even worse for the number of people who keep them up to date. Life changes, and your will should too, to reflect changes in your life or your desires. Have you parents review their wills to be sure that they name the executor they want, and their assets are distributed as they want. If one or both of your parents are in assisted living, have moderate means, or have health conditions, they might also consider drafting their wills so that at the time the first person passes away, their assets go into a "safe harbor trust" for the other, in order to position them to qualify for Medicaid more quickly.

2. <u>Powers of Attorney</u>. A power of attorney document is an extremely important part of estate planning yet one of the most misunderstood. Everyone has been told that it is important to have a will, but for many older people, the most important documents are powers of attorney. They are, quite

frankly, the neglected step-children of estate planning; yet in my practice, they serve to be more important than wills.

Many people confuse the power of attorney (POA) with a will, but these documents are two very different things and have two very different functions. A will goes into effect on the day you die. A POA applies during your lifetime and ceases to apply when you die. So you actually need both a POA and a will as they complement, and do not overlap, each other.

To add a twist to the subject, there are two types of POA's: one for finances and legal matters, and one for health care. These two types are completely separate. They deal with different areas of your life and both are required for effective estate planning.

3. <u>General Durable Power of Attorney or "POA for Legal and Financial Matters"</u>. This POA gives the designated "attorney" – the person you name on the POA document as your decision maker – legal control over all your property. "Property" refers to both real property (real estate) and personal property (all other assets including stocks IRA's, and bank accounts).

The purpose of a POA is to make it easy for your designated attorney to access your finances and, in that way, take care of your property.

The language in the document controls anything the agent can do. As such, it must be carefully drafted according to your desires. Most POA's allow a wide-range of things, including:

paying bills, selling your home, managing investment accounts and IRA's, dealing with the IRS (including signing tax returns).

In all cases, you want to choose someone who is good at managing money to be your POA. Your partner may not be the best choice if you know they have difficulty with money. However, if your partner is trustworthy with money, they may be the perfect choice.

If you don't have a valid financial POA in place and you become incapable, the person who wants to manage your property would need to apply to the courts for the right to do so through a process called a guardianship. Many people call the guardianship a "living probate", and it should be avoided at all cost. The process is time consuming and expensive, especially when compared to the costs of putting a POA for property in place.

4. <u>A Health Care Power of Attorney</u>. A Health Care POA gives your designated attorney the power to make decisions on your behalf in relation to medical issues, hospitalization and long-term care when you are no longer capable of making such decisions yourself. In the case of a POA for personal care, it is a doctor who determines whether you are able to make such decisions.

If you have specific wishes for a particular treatment or plan of care, you can write them directly into your POA document. If your wishes are included in the POA document, or if you have expressed your wishes verbally, your attorney is required by law to make decisions based on those wishes. In the absence of any specific wishes, your attorney is left to make decisions based on what they consider to be your best interests.

Drafting a power of attorney is inexpensive, especially when compared to the expense potentially created by not having one in place when the need arises. Cost should not be a reason for you to postpone the process of creating your POA.

5. <u>A HIPAA Release Waiver</u>. Very often, people want their medical providers to be able to speak with more than just their agent under the POA if they can't speak for themselves. In addition to a health care power of attorney, you can execute a release form that allows other family members to have access to treatment information about you.

6. <u>A Directive to Physicians</u>. This important document allows you to make it plain to those who provide care for you that, in the event you are terminal or in a vegetative state, you don't want your life to be prolonged by artificial means. This often avoids conflict among family members, and reduces the guilt if you are in the situation where that decision has to be made. Although I always recommend you have an attorney draft or review this document for you, there is a wonderful organization that produces a very comprehensive end of life tool called the "5 Wishes". I recommend you take a look at their site: www.agingwithdignity.org.

Financial and estate planning should be considered an essential undertaking for every person who wants to plan ahead for his life. It may take some time to do this but there are lawyers and financial planners who offer their services for a flat fee. It may be time consuming for a busy person but the benefits he and his dependents derive from financial and estate planning makes the time well spent.

One challenge many caregivers have is convincing their parents to undertake planning. Unfortunately, estate planning is optional, and sometimes that effort is unsuccessful. Additionally, very often, parents are unable to undertake planning due to their own incapacity. These, unfortunately, are realities that caregivers often have to deal with. Although it is unpleasant and expensive, a guardianship may be the only option to care for an incapacitated parent who has chosen not to do any planning. Avoiding guardianship should be a goal, as submitting to the courts is not necessarily a favored course of action.

Having a Conversation With Your Parents

Having the "estate planning" conversation can be a very uncomfortable experience. Often, parents are private about their financial affairs and unwilling to volunteer much information. Additionally, children are often uncomfortable bringing up the subject, as they don't want to appear greedy, or overly eager to see their inheritance, and as such, the conversation never takes place.

If your parents are among those with whom that conversation is uncomfortable, it is nevertheless important to start that conversation. The sooner it happens, the better. To the extent possible, talk with your parents gently and honestly about their wishes, their abilities, and their options.

These conversations put you in a better position to make decisions later when your parent may not be able to do so.

Here are some suggestions:

- Share your own feelings and reassure your parent that you will support and help them.

- Help your parent retain whatever control is possible when making his or her own decisions. Respect and try to honor their wishes wherever feasible.

- Encourage the smallest change possible at each step so that your parent is more able to adjust to the change.

- Educate yourself on legal, financial, and medical matters that pertain to your parent as background for your conversations.

- Respect your own needs and be honest with your parents about your time and energy limits.

Making the Conversation Non-Confrontational

Getting together won't do any good unless a conversation takes place. The following phrases are non-confrontational and can help you get the ball rolling:

"I have started to formulate plans in the event something happens to me. What about you?" Personalizing the situation and letting your parents know that you are making plans for yourself allows them to see that you are thinking about your own family.

"What health care measures do you want performed and who should make decisions when you can't?" Asking this question allows a discussion to begin without "money" being the primary topic.

"Have you put your 'final' wishes in writing?" This simple question is one of the best conversation starters. It's not about "who" or "how much," just what your parent wants to happen.

"What steps would you like to take to make sure mom/dad is cared for after you're gone?" This question changes the conversation from "What am I gonna get?" to "I'm concerned about mom/dad's well-being."

"What would you like to have happen to the (insert illiquid asset here)?" Talking about family heirlooms, rather than money, is a much better conversation starter.

Determining Who Takes Responsibility for Aging Parents

When parents become less able to care for themselves, there is a difficult transition from being a child to being a caretaker. During this time of adjustment, it is natural for things to become awkward between you and your parents. After all, it is difficult for both parties to accept that their roles have permanently reversed; now it is the parents who are in need of care, and it is the children who have to provide the caring.

The Proper Time and Place to Discuss Who Takes Responsibility

If you are not an only child, you – or any of your siblings, older or younger – should have a time to meet among all of you, but away from your parents' sight and hearing. This can be a productive time, because you will be discussing several sensitive issues concerning your parents, and these topics may unduly cause pain to your parents if they hear about it.

So...who takes responsibility?

While everyone must take responsibility for caring for one's aging parents, sadly, children in a family may have a range of abilities or interests in caring for parents. Your parents have no doubt dedicated their time, effort, and lives to ensure that all of you have brighter futures to look forward to. They have given you unconditional love and support. It is every child's responsibility to return the gifts they have received from their parents by giving them back the love and care they've been showered with over the years. It is wonderful when all of the children can step-up and help. Unfortunately, that is not always the case, and it is important to be realistic if you find yourself in the position of not having the assistance of siblings.

Responsibilities Must Be Shared

Even though one of your siblings may be willing to shoulder all responsibilities of taking care of your aging parents, this responsibility is better shared by everyone else. Talk and see who among you is better suited to handle which responsibility. Siblings with thriving careers would be more suited to taking care of the financial aspects of caring for aging parents. Those who have lots of free time on their hands can take care of seeing to their parents' business concerns, and other matters that they may no longer have the will or energy to take care of.

Talk to your parents

Once you and your siblings have agreed about who does what and when, it is time to talk to your parents. You must, however, let your parents voice their wishes first to see if their desires coincide with the plans you are about to set in motion. If it doesn't, find a compromise. Remember to be very tactful when discussing this particular topic with your parents; one wrong word and your parents might think you are looking for a way to get rid of them!

Personal care or hired services?

Seeing to your obligations to your parents doesn't necessarily mean that all of you might have to disorganize your lives to personally tend to your parents' care. If you don't think your parents would be hurt with such a decision, you could consider hiring a caregiver or relocate your parents to a higher level of care. Keep in mind, however, that some parents feel they're being abandoned and neglected when their children choose to send them to nursing homes.

Advantages and disadvantages of hiring a caregiver

Pros – You can employ a live-in caregiver for your parents and ensure that all their needs are fully met at whatever time of the day. A caregiver is also equipped to handle a lot of medical and nursing tasks that you may not be presently capable of.

Cons – Having a caregiver can be costly, depending on the wages being asked. Entrusting the lives of your parents to a total stranger is also a big decision to make, especially when it turns out that the caregiver you've hired is irresponsible and/or negligent.

Advantages and disadvantages of skilled nursing

Pros – You'll feel doubly safe with your parents installed in a nursing home because a whole crew of medical professionals is present 24/7, ready to serve all the needs of their patients. Living in a nursing home isn't always sad; it might even be fun once your parents find lots of companions their age to hang out with.

Cons – Besides the expected costs, sending your parents to a nursing home may also constitute as an act of abandonment and betrayal in their eyes.

It is what your parents want and need that counts the most

Although it can get lost in the process, remember, that this is about what your parents want and need. If they are not compliant and you need to step in and become more authoritarian in your approach, try very hard to keep in mind that you must always ask what is in your parents' best interests. No matter how strong, healthy, or rich your parents are, their age is a good indication that they only have a few years left to enjoy their lives. Make it your personal obligation to ensure that they'll retire in utmost comfort and with contentment.

Who Becomes the Caregiver?

Selecting the ideal caregiver for your aging parents

This was discussed briefly in a preceding chapter, but let's explore this subject further. Although nothing in the past can compare to the luxuries that modern technology has gifted us, there's a price to pay for the convenience and comfort it brings: demanding careers, empty social lives, less quality time with our families and even for ourselves, and lastly, the inability to personally care for our aging parents.

Can you act as caregiver for your aging parents?

A caregiver's attention and skills are totally devoted to the elderly patient. Most caregivers that are hired for in-house duties are expected to be able to perform their tasks at any time of the day. They are expected to provide help in all aspects: physical, mental, emotional, and psychological.

A caregiver, in exchange for exerting effort in taking care of the elderly patient, can look forward to receiving hefty compensation. If you are going to act as caregiver for your aging parents, you can't very well expect someone to pay for caring for your OWN parents, can you? So the question is: are you ready and willing to be a caregiver for your aging parents?

The decision to hire a caregiver

At times, however, even though we're perfectly willing to spend most of our time caring for our aging parents, the difficulties of life make it an impractical decision to make. Thus, we are required to hire a caregiver. If we can't take care of our own aging parents, we should at least ensure that the person in charge of providing for our parents' needs is someone who's professionally capable of doing so. That's why you can't just hire anyone who's willing to take care of an aging couple or single for that matter. You need to look for someone who has the right attitude, knowledge, and skills to handle the job competently.

Tips on choosing the ideal caregiver for aging Parents

Parental Participation – Your parents should participate in all parts of the hiring process because they're the ones who'd be most affected if you ended up choosing the wrong person for the job. Ask what your parents are looking for, and encourage them to ask questions.

Recommendations and References – While it is possible for you to find the perfect candidate among all the walk-in applicants you are amenable to entertaining, it is still safer to limit your choices to those who have been recommended by friends, relatives, and agencies, or at the very least, with valid and reliable references. Don't accept references at face value; dial the contact number provided and be sure to ask why the applicant left his previous employ, and a rating or description of the applicant's work attitude and performance.

Experience – If they come with references, these would give you an idea of how much experience these applicants have in providing care to elderly patients. Ask detailed questions about their previous jobs. Hiring an experienced caregiver is better than hiring an inexperienced one, even if it means paying higher wages, simply because you will be able to rest more peacefully at night, knowing that your aging parents are in safe hands.

Skills and Abilities – Have the applicants list all the skills and abilities they possess and that they believe would be useful in caring for elderly patients. If you are looking for a particular skill, now's the time to ask.

Training – Inquire if any of the applicants have received any special training in medical or life-saving techniques and elderly care. A properly trained caregiver would know how to handle elderly patients when they're experiencing a bout of depression or when they're suffering from memory problems.

Attitudes – Test each applicant and see who's impatient, easily angered, or manipulative. As your parents will soon spend most of their time in the caregiver's company, there's a risk that they'll be mistreated when you unknowingly hire an ill-mannered caregiver. This is a very important issue you must address, especially if your parents are already defenseless or handicapped.

Bonding – While you are looking for someone gentle and quiet speaking, your parents may prefer someone who's feisty and blunt. It is best to leave the choice to your parents as they're the ones who'd be spending most of the time with the caregivers anyway.

Choosing the wrong caregiver can actually contribute to shortening your parents' lives. Be careful with your choice, because it is your parents' lives that are at stake!

Accelerating Care Needs

Choosing alternative living arrangements for aging parents

It is always a good thing to plan in advance and anticipate future problems and needs rather than wait for them to arrive. As the days pass by, neither you nor your parents are getting any younger. It is better to plan early regarding long-term care for your parents while they're still healthy and completely able to express their wishes and concerns.

Explaining will prevent parents from getting hurt

Broaching a topic as sensitive as alternative living arrangements and long-term care may cause your parents to entertain misconceptions about the reasons why you are interested in talking about it. Hence, explain to them beforehand that it is because you care for them a lot that you want to prepare and ensure they'll still have a wonderful life once they've reached retirement age.

It is important to listen

A lot of people are unfortunately convinced – albeit having the good intentions – that they know what's better for their parents, even when they don't. Since it is their future at stake, it is logical to ask about their preferences. If you find yourself disagreeing with some of their decisions and suggestions, put yourself in their shoes to know where they're coming from.

Types of alternative living arrangements

If living in the home and hiring a full-time caregiver is out of the question, the following options are still available for your parents' benefit:

Home Care Services: For the right amount and with the right staff, there's no need for your parents to move away home just to benefit from the best of medical care. Although costly, this solution will enable you to personally care for your parents whenever you have the time, and for them to continue enjoying the comfort of familiar surroundings.

Adult Care Program – This type of program ensures that elderly individuals are still able to enjoy active lifestyles. Events, gatherings, and meals that offer social interaction are regularly scheduled for their pleasure. Transportation may also be provided to facilitate the journey to and fro the care center. Other activities such as exercise meetings, games, trips, and concerts are also provided. Several adult care programs may also provide medical assistance if preferred by the individual.

Senior Housing – If your parents are still physically able to sufficiently take care of themselves, and what they want is company and extra care during emergency situations, they may be more suited to living in a retirement or senior home. These facilities are specially designed to assist elderly individuals in their day-to-day activities. At times, meals, transportation and housekeeping can also be arranged, depending on the services offered by the facility.

Federally Subsidized Housing – These housing units are provided by the federal government for the benefit of aging parents from low-income families. While most of these facilities do not offer special care services, a service coordinator is usually left in charge, and may be contacted to for requests of additional services.

Assisted Living – If your parents need less than the attention provided in long-term care programs, but more than what's being given in retirement homes, then they'll no doubt find assisted living the perfect balance. Here, elderly individuals are provided help or assistance only when they want – or need to.

Adult Family Home – Although quality varies greatly between homes, these can be a great options short of skilled nursing. Typically small, with only a few residents, they provide a more "homey" environment for people that feels much less institutional than many skilled nursing facilities.

Continuing-Care Retirement Community – Different types and levels of care are offered in this type of living arrangement. An individual may choose to live in one type of setting for the rest of his stay OR move on to another facility once he's confirmed to have more needs that the facility he's presently living in isn't able to afford.

Skilled Nursing Home – This type of living arrangement is optimal for elderly individuals suffering from chronic diseases. A nursing home ensures that all patients are under round the clock medical supervision to be able to provide instantaneous support.

Memory Care Communities – For people who have dementia and need a secure facility, these can be a godsend. Specially staffed with professionals trained to help people with degenerative memory illnesses, these communities can offer safety and lower stress for your parents.

Factors to Consider Before Choosing an Alternative Arrangement

List Several Places
Organize a list of homes to inquire about and visit. It may be wise to place your name on as many waiting lists as you can as early as possible. Being on a waiting list does not obligate you to move into that particular home, but this advance planning will give you more options when the final decision is being made.

Know Your Needs

You or your loved one may require some special health services: physical, occupational or speech therapy; oxygen, IV therapy or tube feeding; Alzheimer's or young adult services. If you need such services, find out if the home you are looking at provides them--not all homes do. Other issues to consider are the home's location, size and affiliation.

Nursing Home Selection Considerations

Selecting a care provider for a loved one is a difficult task. However, identifying the particular needs of your elderly loved one before beginning the search process will help you explore the available alternatives and make an informed decision. The following Needs Assessment Survey will assist you in your search and prepare you to answer the many questions that will be posed by a facility's staff. Once completed, a summary report may be generated to help you evaluate multiple facilities and expedite the selection process.

Plan to Visit

Plan to visit several nursing homes. This is one of the most important steps in the process; it gives you an opportunity to do some "comparison shopping." Check with the nursing home for scheduled tours, and then make an appointment with the social worker or staff who handles admissions. If you wish, return at a later time for an unannounced visit.

During your visit, USE YOUR FIVE SENSES and let your senses guide you. Trust your instincts. It is OK to do this. If something doesn't feel right to you, it probably isn't. Your senses can help you question such things as:

- Are there unpleasant odors?
- Are the residents well-groomed, dressed and out of bed?
- Is the noise level unusual?
- Does the facility look clean?
- Are staff visible? Friendly?
- Are residents involved in activities?
- Does the home "feel" warm, or impersonal?

When you visit a nursing home, you should carry this checklist with you. It will help you to compare one facility with another, but remember to compare facilities certified in the same category, for example, a skilled nursing facility with another skilled nursing home. Because nursing homes may be licensed in more than one category, always compare similar types of service among facilities.

Look at Daily Life

- Do residents seem to enjoy being with staff?
- Are most residents dressed for the season and time of day?
- Does staff know the residents by name?
- Does staff respond quickly to resident calls for assistance?
- Are activities tailored to residents' individual needs and interests?
- Are residents involved in a variety of activities?
- Does the home serve food attractively?

- Does the home consider personal food likes and dislikes in planning meals?

- Does the home use care in selecting roommates?

- Does the nursing home have a resident's council? If it does, does the council influence decisions [about resident life?

- Does the nursing home have a family council? If it does, does the council influence decisions about resident life?

- Does the facility have contact with community groups, such as pet therapy programs and Scouts?

Look at the Care Residents Receive

- Do various staff and professional experts participate in evaluating each resident's needs and interests?

- Does the resident's family participate in developing the resident's care plan?

- Does the home provide rehabilitation programs, such as physical, occupational, speech and language therapies?

- Does the home have any special services that meet your needs? For example, special care units for residents with dementia or with respiratory problems?

- What is the facility's policy on use of physical/chemical restraints?

- What levels of nursing staff provide care?

- What is the facility's policy on adherence to advanced directives?

Look at the Care Family Caregivers Receive

- Are there programs for family members?
- Are the social service and nursing staff responsive to family members' questions, concerns and needs?
- Would you feel respected by this staff?
- Would you feel like a partner in care with this staff?

Look at How the Nursing Home Handles Payment

- Is the facility certified for Medicare?
- Is the facility certified for Medical Assistance?
- Is the resident or the resident's family informed when charges are increased?
- What are the facility's case mix rates?

Look at the Environment

- Is the outside of the nursing home clean and in good repair?
- Are there outdoor areas accessible for residents to use?
- Is the inside of the nursing home clean and in good repair?
- Does the nursing home have handrails in hallways and grab bars in bathrooms?
- When floors are being cleaned, are warning signs displayed, or are areas blocked off to prevent accidents?
- Is the nursing home free from unpleasant odors?
- Are toilets convenient to bedrooms?
- Do noise levels fit the activities that are going on
- Is it easy for residents in wheelchairs to move around the home?
- Is the lighting appropriate for what residents are doing?
- Are there private areas for residents to visit with family, visitors, or physicians?
- Are residents' bedrooms furnished in a pleasant manner?
- Do the residents have some personal items in their bedrooms (for example, family pictures, souvenirs, a chair)?
- Do the residents' rooms have accessible storage areas for residents' personal items?

Other Things to Note

- Does the nursing home have a good reputation in the community?
- Is there a specific affiliation?
- Does the nursing home have a list of references?
- Is the nursing home convenient for family or friends to visit?
- Do you have questions or concerns? If so, call the local or state Long-Term Care Ombudsman Program.
- Does your family member's physician have a relationship with this facility?

Choosing an alternative living arrangement for your parents is going to be a big decision. Hence, take as much time as you want or need, because your choice can help your parents have a pleasant – or tortuous – future.

What to Do When Aging Parents Need Long-Term Care

Seeing formerly healthy parents forced to depend on the care of other people and unable to function on their own is a painful sight to witness for any child. Being unable to provide the necessary medical and financial aid however is more painful to bear. While you've a steady income to rely on, consider planning ahead and saving for your parents' future needs...before it is too late.

The Difference between Traditional and Long-Term Medical Care

We have discussed the various methods for caring for your parent(s) in the previous chapters.

However, there's more to worry about when your parents are in need of long-term medical care. Traditional medical care is usually provided when aging individuals are in need of temporary medical assistance; traditional medical care is provided to help a person recover, or rehabilitate or correct his injuries. Long-term care is provided, on the other hand, on a permanent basis; people who are diagnosed as having a chronic ailment are those in need of long-term care. Long-term care ensures that all the wants and needs that a seriously ill and aging individual is no longer capable of meeting are fully addressed by the person in charge.

Paying for Long-Term Care

Who looks forward to living in a nursing home? Few people build the possibility into their financial planning, an understandable lapse, but unwise in the long run. Even if they did, the cold fact is that the options available to pay for long-term care, whether it is a nursing home, an assisted living facility, or home care, are limited and too often unaffordable.

Still, it is a harsh reality that about 70 percent of 65-year-olds will need long-term care at some point, according to a study conducted by researchers at Penn State, Georgetown, and the Lewin Group. Of that group, about 30 percent will need it for more than five years. That's extreme—the average long-term stay is about 2½ years. But it is expensive even for short-timers. Depending on the state and community, skilled nursing can range between $4500 and $13,000 per month.

Other long-term care options are less onerous but will still wreck many fixed incomes. Assisted living facilities, where people who don't need skilled nursing care can get help with essential but routine chores, are much less expensive, averaging $36,372 annually. For those who can stay put, the services of a home health aide typically cost $20 an hour. Adult day care, another option that can allow someone to continue to live at home with family, costs $64 per day on average, in 2012.

Medicare isn't an option for true long-term care. Coverage of skilled nursing care is limited to 100-day benefit periods and requires at least three days of hospitalization before being admitted to a home. It is fine for someone who's just had surgery or an acute case of pneumonia and needs recovery or rehabilitation, but it is no answer for someone with Alzheimer's disease or a debilitating chronic condition. Moreover, "covered" doesn't mean free. While Medicare pays all expenses for the first 20 days, the next 80 cost a resident $133.50 a day—that is, if coverage for the full 100 days is approved; consumer advocates say approval for much shorter stays is more likely. Medicare will also cover an unlimited number of days of part-time home healthcare for homebound seniors, although again, getting approval can be difficult. Medicare will not cover care in assisted living facilities.

There's no one right answer. The best option for a particular individual will take into account income and assets, current health, family medical history, and whether family members can pitch in to help. Geography also plays a role—nursing home costs vary widely, from $566 per day for a semiprivate room in Alaska to just $121 in parts of Minnesota and Oklahoma.

It is never too early to begin weighing your options from among the four major sources for funding long-term care:

Paying out of pocket

Self-funding is for the financially fortunate. It is especially attractive to those who don't wish to buy long-term care insurance (see below) or who would be turned down for medical reasons. It hardly needs to be said that reasonably substantial assets that provide steady cash flow are necessary. "Substantial" depends on where you live, among other things, but generally it means at least a few hundred thousand dollars. If you have a good income from a pension and Social Security or investments, you could be fine.

Buying long-term care insurance

A long-term care policy pays a specified daily amount for nursing home care for a specified number of years or for the policyholder's lifetime. It typically covers care in other settings as well, such as the home or an assisted living facility.

Many experts are lukewarm about such insurance. The policies are complicated, the language is often confusing, and the Oracle itself would be baffled by the significant decisions that must be made. Take timing. Is it better to buy at a younger age, when premiums are cheaper, recognizing that you will likely write premium checks for decades before you need to tap the coverage—if you ever do? Or is it wiser to wait and buy when coverage is more expensive but you are closer to when you will need it? A policy that pays out $100 a day for three years would cost an average 55-year-old $709 in annual premiums, according to the American Association for Long-Term Care Insurance. That same policy would cost a typical 65-year-old $1,342. If your family is stocked with hale and hearty 85-year-old marathoners, you may want to delay. On the other hand, if cancer runs in your family, you might want to consider buying on the earlier side. And although three years of coverage may be enough for an average long-term stay, are you willing to risk the possibility that you will need five or 10 years?

Uses of Insurance and Annuities for Long-Term Care Costs

Sound alternatives to either self-paying for long-term care costs or accessing Medicaid by transferring assets to loved ones include the purchase of insurance and annuities. This means that the advice of an experienced financial adviser is strongly recommended in addition to the advice of an elder law attorney.

The quality and coverage of long-term care (LTC) insurance has improved as a result of the enactment of the Health Insurance Portability and Accountability Act of 1996 (HIPAA). LTC policies qualified under HIPAA require coverage not only for traditional nursing home costs, but also for home health care, assisted living and dementia-type diseases. A portion of premiums paid for policies qualified under federal HIPAA guidelines is a tax-deductible medical expense on Schedule A of the 1040 return.

A disabled person covered under LTC insurance can have access to better LTC choices, including:

- A higher-quality nursing home
- A better chance to stay at home with home health coverage
- Intermediate and assisted living facilities

In addition to these advantages, LTC insurance provides asset protection for the at-home spouse, as well as the ultimate beneficiaries when both parents have passed away.

An alternative to LTC insurance is life insurance. After a nursing home resident dies, the life insurance proceeds can be used to replace the wealth lost to pay long-term care costs. More life insurance companies offer nursing home riders on life insurance policies, which allow distributions of benefits to pay for nursing home costs, if it becomes necessary.

An Introduction Techniques to Qualify for Medicaid

A person facing the prospect of long-term care with moderate income and assets may eventually have to rely on Medicaid to pay part or all of the cost of care. In the Medicaid chapter we learn of provisions to protect a healthy spouse financially. But many states rob a healthy spouse of a previously adequate income by allowing too little in protected resources and income. Likewise, children, relatives and friends are not recognized for the financial sacrifices they make in providing the early care before a recipient becomes bad enough to need Medicaid funded professional help.

Medicaid planning, using a professional Medicaid planning advisor or qualified elder law attorney, allows you to correct inequities in the system. Medicaid planning has gotten a bad name because some individuals, who would normally have too many assets to ever qualify for Medicaid, deliberately use it, many years in advance, to give away everything to their family so as to qualify for Medicaid. It is wrong to abuse the system in this way and to use taxpayer dollars to insure an inheritance for the family. And if that person is not anticipating immediate care, this strategy is just plain dumb.

Our own experience with Medicaid planning, with families that attend our elder care planning workshops, is that there is no intent to take advantage of the system. In almost all cases the family is confronting an immediate need for long-term care and there is usually not enough money to pay for it out of pocket. They are looking for advice on how to get Medicaid to cover that care. Most families using Medicaid planning have very little assets to begin with. Most are simply concerned with keeping the house in the family. Children have seen their parents struggle to preserve and have pride in an asset they can call their own and possibly pass on to children. To be thwarted in trying to preserve the family home because of Medicaid recovery just doesn't seem right somehow.

Families feel the same about the small amount of savings that parents have accumulated over the years. It seems unjust to families to wipe out these accounts when other government health services don't require a sacrifice of assets. And indeed, the concept of Medicaid recovery seems to be only unique to Medicaid services.

Federal disaster relief, crop protection, Medicare services, aging services and programs for low income individuals do not require families to hand over their assets after the recipient dies. Or what if people live in a flood zone but can't afford flood insurance. If rising waters from a hurricane completely destroy their property and the federal government helps them rebuild that property, the government is not going to confiscate the home after they die. If people fail to insure for long-term care and Medicaid pays for that care, why does the government have the right to confiscate their property?

Some Medicaid planners will attempt to discredit other forms of funding long-term care such as using insurance or a reverse mortgage. They do this in order to discourage the public from using these other strategies. The intent is to limit competition ensuring that paying clients will rely entirely on Medicaid planning as a solution. On the other hand, many long term care funding specialists will use the same strategy against Medicaid planners to eliminate competition from their services. These people make Medicaid planners appear as evil or dishonest. Medicaid planning is no different from tax planning. In fact a Supreme Court decision condones honest methods of eliminating income taxes or estate taxes. Tax planning and Medicaid planning both put an additional burden on taxpayers, but one is considered ethical and the other not.

I believe that all strategies have their place in the scheme of things. Medicaid planning fits certain circumstances usually where families are in a crisis mode trying to preserve a few assets such as a house or a savings plan. There is no attempt to take advantage of the taxpayers. Using other strategies for paying the cost of care is much better for a younger generation wanting a plan that will allow for home care, assisted living and a choice in care services.

It is also important to consider that most states resist the concept of Medicaid recovery either overtly or discreetly. In fact one state, West Virginia, refused to institute it until threatened by the federal government. Politically, state governments appear to be particularly hardhearted in taking away a widow's home after she dies or in depriving a poor family of a possible means of improving their situation by taking away their family assets. States do a miserable job in their recovery efforts. Secretly most states probably prefer Medicaid planners taking the heat for preserving family assets.

Below are a few of the strategies used to protect income and assets. Since Medicaid rules vary from state to state, you need to talk to a qualified planner or elder law attorney in your state to see the range of planning tools that can be used for your particular situation.

Income Annuity in the Name of the Community Spouse

This technique relies on two Medicaid rules. The first rule is that income between couples is attributed to the spouse who owns the income. Unlike assets which have to be shared for Medicaid eligibility, income does not have to be shared. For example if the Medicaid recipient has a total income of $500 a month and the community spouse has a total income of $4000 a month the community spouse is not required to contribute any income towards the care of his or her spouse. Medicaid will cover the bill less the $500 a month, which less a monthly allowance must be spent towards the cost of care. The second rule allows a spouse to transfer any amount of assets to another spouse without penalty of losing Medicaid eligibility.

Using these two rules, here is how a Medicaid annuity strategy works

The person needing long-term care -- the institutional spouse -- applies to Medicaid in order to receive Medicaid services. In this case suppose the couple has $100,000 of cash equivalent assets and owns a home and a car. As long as the healthy spouse -- the community spouse -- lives in the home she can keep the home and the car and those assets do not prevent the institutional spouse from receiving Medicaid help. In this example, the institutional spouse must spend $50,000 of the couple's assets down to less than $2000 and have an income insufficient to cover the cost of care and then Medicaid will take over.

Once the Medicaid application has been approved, instead of starting the spend down to $2,000 and then having Medicaid pick up the balance of the cost, the institutional spouse transfers his $50,000 to his wife. This is allowable and will not disqualify the Medicaid approval process but it does not yet take away the responsibility to spend down the cash. The community spouse then uses the money to purchase an immediate income annuity for a period equal to or less than the allowable life expectancy in the HCFA transmittal 64 table. Assets have now been converted to about $800 a month in income. The income belongs to the community spouse and does not have to be shared with the institutional spouse. Therefore the spend down as been avoided. Evidence of this transaction is presented to Medicaid and because the institutional spouse no longer has any attributable assets, Medicaid starts paying its share of the bill.

This strategy serves two purposes. First, it may give the community spouse a larger income than she otherwise would have had under Medicaid rules. Second, even though it represents income, the community spouse has managed to keep $50,000 that would normally have to be spent.

In the past, some planners have set up annuities that provide a remainder payout should the community spouse die too soon. This is usually paid to the children and in the past was used as a way to transfer assets to the children without penalty. Under the Deficit Reduction Act of 2006, the state must be named as beneficiary for any remainder payout. This new rule discourages the use of these annuities to transfer assets to the next generation.

It is important for the planner to follow Medicaid guidelines in transmittal 64 in order to avoid a penalty. If the payout period of the annuity exceeds the life expectancy in Medicaid tables, then the excess amount of total income payment over the life expectancy becomes a transfer for less than value and represents a penalty. This in turn results in a penalty period equal to the amount of excess divided by the monthly Medicaid rate in that state. Medicaid will not start paying for care until this penalty period has been met with someone else paying for that care. We have included the transmittal 64 table below. Medicaid annuities are also required to be irrevocable and it is preferable to make them nonassignable. It is important to use a qualified adviser to make sure you do all of this properly.

Section of Transmittal 64 Dealing With Annuities (Medicaid Annuities)

The law provides that the term "trust" includes an annuity to the extent and in such manner as the Secretary specifies. This subsection describes how annuities are treated under the trust/transfer provisions.

When an individual purchases an annuity, he or she generally pays to the entity issuing the annuity (e.g., a bank or insurance company) a lump sum of money, in return for which he or she is promised regular payments of income in certain amounts. These payments may continue for a fixed period of time (for example, 10 years) or for as long as the individual (or another designated beneficiary) lives, thus creating an ongoing income stream. The annuity may or may not include a remainder clause under which, if the annuitant dies, the contracting entity converts whatever is remaining in the annuity into a lump sum and pays it to a designated beneficiary.

Annuities, although usually purchased in order to provide a source of income for retirement, are occasionally used to shelter assets so that individuals purchasing them can become eligible for Medicaid. In order to avoid penalizing annuities validly purchased as part of a retirement plan but to capture those annuities which abusively shelter assets, a determination must be made with regard to the ultimate purpose of the annuity (i.e., whether the purchase of the annuity constitutes a transfer of assets for less than fair market value). If the expected return on the annuity is commensurate with a reasonable estimate of the life expectancy of the beneficiary, the annuity can be deemed actuarially sound.

Proper Use of Medicaid Annuities

It is important to use the services of a qualified Medicaid planner or elder law attorney when implementing Medicaid income annuities. The annuity must follow "HCFA Transmittal 64" guidelines or it may be challenged and disqualified as a "transfer for less than value" by your state Medicaid.

Some states have established rules against the use of Medicaid annuities even though Federal Medicaid law and Federal guidelines condone their use. State disallowance of Medicaid annuities has been challenged in several court cases with the States in question being judged on the wrong side of the issue. On the other hand if your state disallows Medicaid annuities it is best for you not to do one than to end up incurring the costs of an expensive legal battle.

When Annuities Should Not Be Used

The two most serious pitfalls that annuity salespeople often fail to disclose are that income received by a Medicaid recipient from an annuity will be paid to the nursing home, and that there will be an attempt at estate recovery in those states which have estate recovery against income annuities.

There is also concern about the improper sale to the elderly of an allied vehicle called a deferred annuity. Congress allowed the deferred accumulation, annuity vehicle as a means for holding or accumulating money, tax deferred, until it would be annuitized into retirement income in a person's later years. It makes great sense for a 55 year old person at the peak of his or her earning years to purchase a deferred annuity for a period of 10 years with the idea of converting it to income after he or she retires and would be in a lower income tax bracket.

It makes much less sense for a 70-year-old widow in a 15 percent tax bracket to purchase a deferred annuity with the idea of deferring income until a later date. What often happens instead is that the annuity cash account accumulates deferred taxable earnings and instead of being converted to income, money is taken out in a lump sum. First dollars taken out of deferred annuities are treated as earnings and tax due on these lump sum surrenders is likely to push the owner's 15 percent tax rate into a higher bracket. Also, early surrenders from deferred annuities within the first 7 to 10 years result in surrender penalties of 1% to 10%. These penalties are rarely disclosed by annuity sales people.

Deferred annuities are also a lousy way to create an inheritance. Unlike stocks, bonds or property which receive a step-up in basis on the death of the shareholder (results in zero taxes to the heirs), there is no step-up in basis for the income which has been accumulated in a deferred annuity. Eventually, this income must be distributed and the tax paid by the heirs. The longer the income accumulates, the larger it becomes and the larger the ultimate tax bite.

Unfortunately, there are firms that aggressively market annuities improperly to seniors. These organizations often conduct marketing seminars under the guise of educating the attendees about financial issues affecting senior citizens. The advertisements contain scare tactics and false and misleading information. While some of the underlying information might be truthful, it is often presented in a sensational manner. All of this is done with the intention of persuading the senior citizen into purchasing a deferred annuity. Some annuity salesmen make as much as $500,000 to $1,000,000 a year in deferred annuity sales commissions.

In addition, in these sales seminars, the income tax benefits of deferring income are usually exaggerated, the surrender charges for early withdrawal are usually glossed over if mentioned at all, the appropriateness of the annuity for the age of the purchaser is rarely discussed, and the attendees are misinformed that the purchase of the annuity will help protect the asset from subsequent claims of a nursing home. The details as to how the annuity needs to be structured for Medicaid eligibility, however, are rarely mentioned. Finally, the overall disadvantages of annuity ownership are never raised.

Prepaid Funeral Instead of or in Addition to Burial Funds

Federal rules allow a person on Medicaid to keep up to $1,500 for funeral expenses. Most states allow a recipient to buy a prepaid funeral plan. The limit for such a plan is always higher than the $1,500 allowed by Federal rules. As an example, if your state allows $7,000 for a prepaid funeral plan then you should use the full amount you have money for to buy a plan.

Your state may also allow additional costs such as the burial plots, caskets and vaults to be tacked on, thus raising the limit.

Use of Spend Down Resources

People assume money being spent down for Medicaid eligibility needs to be applied to care costs. In reality, Medicaid is only interested in seeing the potential Medicaid recipient's resources reduced to less than $2,000. How the money is spent is only questioned if there has been a transfer for less than value.

In order to qualify for Medicaid more quickly, you may want to use some of the spend down money to pay off debt, trade in the old car and buy a new one. (Medicaid typically allows a community spouse to retain just one car), or fix up the house.

Intend to Return Home

If a single person receiving Medicaid care in a facility has a house, that property could be subject to sale to pay for Medicaid expenses. The house is only protected if a qualifying child or dependent lives there or if the recipient intends on returning home. Some states require a medical doctor to certify a return home, but in many states it only requires the signature of the recipient whether that recipient has justification or not. In the states that allow it, always have your loved one sign an intent to return home. At least you have use of the property while your loved one is still alive.

Medicaid treatment of a Home

If the community spouse lives in the home then the home is exempt from determining Medicaid eligibility. It does not count as an asset and prevent the institutional spouse from receiving Medicaid help. On the other hand any other real estate property, not the primary residence, will have to be converted to cash and spent down before Medicaid will start paying the bill.

If the community spouse living in the home does not in turn need Medicaid help in the future then one of two things can happen to the house after the death of the institutional spouse. Legally Medicaid has a claim against the property for recovery services. And in some states a lien against the property, called a TEFRA lien, can be filed in anticipation of Medicaid's cost. The lien can be filed before the death of the care recipient but only a few states actually do that. States that have authority to file these liens often don't so until after the death. At the death of the community spouse, the property cannot be sold until the lien is satisfied. But in states where there is no lien, if the community spouse dies after the institutional spouse it is unlikely that state Medicaid recovery will use the property as an asset for recovery.

And in many states if the property is inside a trust, the state may not consider the house an asset for recovery even though most states have altered their definition of estate to include a trust. Many states still rely on filing a claim in probate court to initiate recovery. The bottom line is very few states are efficient at recovery especially when it comes to a primary residence. Always contact and work with a competent adviser when dealing with recovery issues. You can never assume what your state recovery program will actually do.

Special Home Exemption Rule

It is often the case that a daughter will move in to take care of Mom or Dad or both. In this case Medicaid has a special leniency rule to allow transfer of the home to the daughter and not result in a penalty for a transfer for less than value. If the child provides care for a parent in a parent's home for at least two years, and that care kept the recipient out of a nursing home, the property can be transferred to the child without penalty and the property will not be a subject asset for Medicaid recovery. Medicaid will require some proof of this. Typically an affidavit from a third-party care provider such as a doctor or an agency stipulating that the care was given for at least two years and resulted in keeping the care recipient out of a long-term care facility, will be sufficient evidence. It is important to use a legal adviser to make sure you do this properly.

Joint Tenancy

Some states, in estate recovery, only go after property that goes through probate. Property titled in joint tenancy with rights of survivorship passes at death to the living tenant and avoids probate. If the title is in joint tenancy or held in trust and the joint tenant or beneficiary, at death, changes title before the state files its lien then the state could have no legal claim against the property.

On the other hand, state recovery does not go after property itself but simply requires repayment of Medicaid costs based on assets a Medicaid recipient held prior to applying for Medicaid. The family is responsible for coming up with the money based on the value of the assets. It is very likely, however, in most states that property passing in joint tenancy will simply escape Medicaid recovery or assessment because recovery services may not even be aware of the death of the care recipient until the property has passed in ownership. At that point it could become a legal challenge between state recovery and the family and possibly for bad publicity the state may forgo any further legal action. On the other hand, as Medicaid budgets become stretched, states may become more aggressive in recovery tactics that the law allows them.

Many people anticipating Medicaid services are tempted to put a child's or sibling's name on property titles to avoid probate and Medicaid recovery. It may not be a good idea.

There are at least four problems with putting a child's name on an asset

- If the other person on the title becomes subject to a judgment, even one arising from an accident, then at least 50% of the property can be lost to the judgment.

- The other person on the title must consent to any disposition of the property. He or she might not be in accordance with what the original owner wants to do.

- Redoing the title must occur at least 5 years prior to claim in order to avoid look back rules and a sanction on a gift to a non- spouse owner.

- The person assuming joint ownership has received a gift and loses the step-up in basis at death. Capital gains taxes may have to be paid. And if the property is not the principal residence of the new tenant, the capital gains exclusion cannot be used either.

Transfer Title of the Property to the Community Spouse

Transfers to a spouse of any assets are exempt from Medicaid eligibility rules. An institutional spouse, anticipating Medicaid, can transfer title in the home to the community spouse and it has no effect on Medicaid eligibility. This can be done either with a quit claim deed or through a trust. With the asset no longer in the name of the care recipient, Medicaid recovery cannot use the house as a basis for recovering its costs. And the community spouse can transfer the house to a member of the family and as long as this is done beyond the three-year look back period, then Medicaid can't assess a penalty period for a transfer of assets for less than value if the transferring spouse eventually needs Medicaid services. It is important to use a legal adviser to make sure you do this properly.

Trust to Avoid Probate

Common trusts to avoid probate are called "living" or "inter vivos" trusts. A trust never dies, thus it is not subject to probate. Most arrangements make the trust the owner of the property with the original owner(s) as trustee(s) (caretaker as it were) and beneficiaries(s). Thus the property reverts to the estate at death. Most people initiate these trusts to avoid probate. Assets in these trusts, other than a primary residence, are transparent to Medicaid. These trust assets are subject to Medicaid spend down rules.

The trust can be used in states where Medicaid recovery only uses primary residences passing through a probate as being subject to recovery. However, a growing number of states do not recognize these arrangements to avoid probate estate recovery and go after primary residences in revocable trusts regardless of ownership.

To do it right for these states requires an irrevocable trust with no life interest, set up 5 years or more before a Medicaid claim. Very few people are willing to do these kinds of trusts.

Some people also include a so-called "life interest" in property in arrangements where property is gifted or in irrevocable trusts. The life interest gives them use of the property until their death even though they don't own it. Medicaid in many states does not recognize life interest and the property is considered to be in the ownership of the person who gifted it and subject to look back rules and recovery.

Move Loved One Needing Care to another State

A person needing Medicaid covered care in one state may not qualify under that state's rules but might qualify under the rules of a neighboring state. Of particular concern are candidates suffering from dementia or Alzheimer's. It is difficult to quantify their need for care and in some states, those people who are cognitively impaired might not get help with Medicaid even though their needs might be greater than the needs of those who are physically disabled.

Families should consider moving loved ones who have been declined in one state, to live with a member of the family in another state and possibly qualifying in that state. In addition the new state may be more lenient with Medicaid recovery procedures.

Gifting Assets

We have already discussed the moral implications of using Medicaid planning strategies for unfairly qualifying for Medicaid and shifting the burden of cost to the taxpayers. New look back rules under the deficit reduction act have effectively done away with gifting strategies used in the past to accelerate eligibility for Medicaid. This does not mean that gifts cannot be used, but planning must be done many years in advance. Under these new circumstances the whole concept of gifting in order to qualify for Medicaid probably makes little sense.

Veterans Long Term Care Benefits

The Veterans Administration offers an amazing benefit to veterans. "Aid and attendance" is a commonly used term for a little-known veterans' long-term care benefit. The official title of this benefit is "The VA Modern Pension." The reason for using "aid and attendance" to refer to Pension is that many veterans or their single surviving spouses can become eligible if they have a regular need for the aid and attendance of a caregiver or if they are housebound. Evidence of this need for care must be certified by VA as a "rating." With a rating, certain veterans or their surviving spouses can now qualify for Pension.

The purpose of this benefit is to provide supplemental income to disabled or older veterans who have a low income or high medical costs. Pension is for war veterans who have disabilities that are not connected to their active-duty service. Pension is primarily intended for lower income veterans, but a special provision in how Pension is calculated can allow veterans or single surviving spouses with higher income to also receive the benefit which may be as much as $2,200 a month. This special provision kicks in for veterans who have ongoing and expensive long term care costs.

Aid and Attendance Pension benefit can pay up to $2,200 a month for qualifying long term care needs such as:

- Family members to provide home care
- Professional home care providers to come into your home
- Assisted Living or Adult Day services
- Nursing Home long term care
- Home renovations for disability

In 2012, the following are the maximums paid, depending upon the situation

- Married couple: $2,200/month ($26,400/year)
- Single Veteran: $1,704/month ($20,448/year)
- Surviving Spouse: $1,094/month ($13,128/year)
- Spouse of a Living Veteran: $1,338/month ($16,056/year)

If the veteran's income exceeds the pension amount, there is usually no award given, however, income can be adjusted for unreimbursed medical expenses (UME), and this allows veterans without household incomes larger than the Pension amount to qualify for a monthly benefit. There is also an asset test to qualify for Pension.

An Overview of the VA Pension Benefit

Pension is a benefit paid to <u>wartime veterans</u> who have <u>limited or no income</u>, and who age 65 or older are, or, if under 65, who are permanently and totally disabled. Veterans who are more seriously disabled may qualify for <u>Aid and Attendance or Housebound</u> benefits. These are benefits that are paid in addition to the basic pension rate.

Generally, you may be eligible if:

- you were discharged from service under conditions other than dishonorable,

AND

- You served at least 90 days of active military service 1 day of which was during a war time period. If you entered active duty after September 7, 1980, generally you must have served at least 24 months or the full period for which called or ordered to active duty (There are exceptions to this rule),

AND

- your <u>countable</u> family income is below a yearly limit set by law (The yearly <u>limit on income</u> is set by Congress),

AND

- You are age 65 or older, OR, you are permanently and totally disabled, not due to your own willful misconduct.

As you can see, there are a number of criteria that may affect your eligibility to pension benefits. If you are unsure if you meet all criteria, we encourage you to go ahead and file an application, particularly if you have countable income that appears to be near the maximum.

VA will determine if you are eligible and notify you. If you do not initially qualify, you may reapply if you have un-reimbursed medical expenses during the twelve month period after VA receives your claim that bring your countable income below the yearly income limit. (These are expense you have paid for medical services or products for which you will not be reimbursed by Medicare or private medical insurance.)

This includes income received by the veteran and his or her dependents, if any, from most sources. It includes earnings, disability and retirement payments, interest and dividends, and net income from farming or business.

What about net worth?

Net worth means the net value of the assets of the veteran and his or her dependents. It includes such assets as bank accounts, stocks, bonds, mutual funds and any property other than the veteran's residence and a reasonable lot area. There is no set limit on how much net worth a veteran and his dependents can have, but net worth cannot be excessive. Although the maximum is $80,000 for couples and $40,000 for single people, the VA lowers this acceptable amount based upon the age of the individual applying. As such, a veteran in his 80's would be allowed less than a veteran in his 60's.

The decision as to whether a claimant's net worth is excessive depends on the facts of each individual case. All net worth should be reported and VA will determine if a claimant's assets are sufficiently large that the claimant could live off these assets for a reasonable period of time. VA's needs-based programs are not intended to protect substantial assets or build up an estate for the benefit of heirs.

Transfers to Family and to Trusts

Unlike with Medicaid, there are currently no look back periods or ineligibility periods for transfers into trust or to children. This must be done very carefully, and under the supervision of a qualified elder law attorney, or you run the risk of jeopardizing both your VA benefits and possible Medicaid benefits in the future. Oftentimes, the need for care grows progressively, and the veteran is placed in the position of needing Medicaid benefits. If the veteran has transferred assets in order to qualify for VA benefits without due consideration of Medicaid look back periods, it could cause the veteran to be ineligible for Medicaid. Consequently, due care and concern must be given to whether a transfer of assets is prudent in each individual case.

Caring for Older Relatives

While annuities *may* be a valuable part of a good financial plan, there is no requirement that you purchase an annuity in order to qualify for the benefit. If you establish a trust, the trust can own any assets including real estate, CD's, stocks, and checking accounts.

Your home is not a countable resource, so you don't have to transfer your home to qualify. If you are planning to sell your home, however, it may make great sense to ask a qualified elder law attorney to put your home into a trust. If you do so, then the proceeds of the sale of the home won't jeopardize your VA benefit. Additionally, a transfer of the home may start the look back period running for Medicaid purposes, which may or may not be a good idea, depending upon your own situation.

You may apply for Aid and Attendance or Housebound benefits by writing to the VA Regional office having jurisdiction of the claim. That would be the office where you filed a claim for pension benefits. If the regional office of jurisdiction is not known, you may file the request with any VA Regional office.

You can apply on line at the following VA web site:

http://vabenefits.vba.va.gov/vonapp/main.asp .

You may download and fill out VA Form 21-526, Veteran's Application for Compensation and/or Pension. Make sure you download all parts of the application as well as the instructions for filling out the forms.

If available, attach copies of dependency records (marriage & children's birth certificates).

You must send the completed application and any copies of other documents to the VA regional office that serves your area of residence.

You may also contact a Veterans Service Officer (VSO) from a veteran's service organization. Please call the toll free number, 1-800-827-1000, for the location of the nearest VSO nearest you. You may also look to the VA web site for a list of the nationally recognized Veterans Service Organizations.

There are also accredited lawyers, claims agents and private services that will assist with the application.

The VA says that approval takes 6-8 months, but if everything is in order and the application is done properly the first time, approval sometimes comes in 4 months or less. You receive payments retroactive to the date of application, so when approval does come, there is usually a fairly large check for the months spent waiting.

Medical Care for Older Adults

Tips on Providing Medical Care for Aging Parents

Taking good care of aging parents is a difficult job, but if you love your parents, you must double your efforts to prevent any chances of them getting harmed. Your parents are growing older each day, and you owe it to them to make their last days as comfortable and pleasant as possible. One way of doing so is ensuring that your parents are given the best of medical care.

Love Cures

Before we set about discussing the finer details of providing medical care for aging parents, be sure that you always show your love for them through your words and actions. No matter how much you work hard to give them the best medical treatments that money can afford, all of these will be considered meaningless if your parents feel that you are doing them only out of obligation or pity and not out of love, and a genuine wish to see them happy.

Aging parents are also very vulnerable to depression because they find it hard to come to terms with their gradually increasing dependency on other people. Even if you've heard your parents' complaints for the hundredth time, never show that you are fed up listening. Think of it this way, if you will: what's an hour's worth of listening to your parents rant when it means they'll be able to sleep peacefully through the night, knowing that you care about what they think and feel?

Research Diligently about the Medical Condition

Whatever it is that's ailing your parents, you must make it your goal to know as much as possible about the disease. That way, you will be mentally, psychologically, and emotionally equipped to handle any medical emergencies if you happen to be alone during a sudden attack.

Consider Hiring a Caregiver

If your aging parents still refuse to live in a nursing home or any other similar facility where they'll be properly attended to, consider hiring a caregiver, if not full-time, then at least during those instances that you are not at home. Also, upon hiring a caregiver, consider giving him the authority to make decisions regarding your parents when you are not present and during emergencies.

Keep a Copy of Medical Records

Even though your parents are meticulous when it comes to their medical records and other related documents, there's no harm in keeping an extra copy. This will ensure that no matter what happens information about your parents' health is readily accessible.

Know the Schedule of Doctor and Hospital Appointments of Your Parents

Some parents can be very lazy about keeping their appointments with their doctors. The simple act of missing an appointment however can sometimes be the sole reason why your parents weren't given proper medication or treatment. Whether your parents like it or not, assign yourself as their personal event organizer. Keep a detailed list of their appointments and make sure they not only keep their appointments, but that they're also there on time.

Accompanying Parents to Medical Appointments

If you are unable to accompany your parents to a scheduled appointment, make sure that someone reliable will stand in your stead. Elderly individuals often have impaired vision and hearing, which may make them miss out on an important instruction or two.

Having a companion with them will ensure that this won't happen at any rate.

Providing Emotional Support

Simple medical tests which we take in stride may be especially painful physically and emotionally for elderly individuals. A blood test, for instance, is more painful to administer because elderly people have thinner skins and more fragile veins. Such medical tests are also visible reminders that serve to emphasize what they're going through and what they've lost because of their conditions. Your presence will no doubt alleviate the pain that your parents might be feeling at the moment.

Ensure Prompt Payment of Insurance Fees and Other Medical Bills

If your parents aren't insured, take the necessary steps to make them so. Also, pay your parents' bills on time. Having a high balance of debt might cause delay in giving proper care to your parents, something none of you could afford to happen during cases of life and death.

Lastly, before trying anything new for your parents, always consult their personal physician. Although you mean well, good intentions are not a guarantee for safety.

Nutritional Needs for older people

Knowing What the Right Foods Are for Aging Parents

It is not enough to provide your aging parents with the best medical treatments and shower them with love and affection. If you really care about their health, you need to be firm about what they can and cannot eat. Prepare yourself for daily battles though; as people get older, they tend to become more stubborn, irritable, and taciturn and your parents would surely never give up their favorite fast food meals and deliciously fatty steaks without a fight!

Malnourishment Has an Invisible Presence

That's something you have to understand early on. Even though your parents still seem to be enjoying the peak of health, and have a fun and active lifestyle, there's a good chance that they're malnourished if they're eating the wrong food. To know whether your parents are malnourished or not, schedule them for an appointment with their personal physician or a nutritionist. It is time for your folks to face the music!

Possible Causes of Malnutrition

There are several reasons why your parents may arrive at a state of malnutrition and some of the most common reasons have been listed below:

Alcoholism, Smoking and Drugs – If your parents are guilty of indulging any of these hazardous vices, know that these greatly contribute to the state of malnutrition that your parents find themselves in right now.

Depression – A lot of people find it difficult to adjust with their increasing age, an attitude which consequently makes them lose their appetite. Also, elderly individuals who feel they've been abandoned by their loved ones commonly suffer from similar effects.

Medication – Taking too much medication, especially without the advice and permission from a physician, can also make an aging individual malnourished.

Special Dietary Needs

Besides the basic nutritional needs of the elderly, your parents may be required to adhere to other dietary restrictions if they're diagnosed as suffering from diabetes, high blood pressure, or other similarly dangerous conditions. Again, a trip to the hospital would easily reveal the truth about your parents' health.

Basic Nutritional Needs of Older People

Fat – This particular food group has never been good for any age group, much less for those past their prime. If, however, an individual is over 75, or is suffering from weight loss or lack of appetite, including fat in the person's diet will actually be beneficial as it contributes to weight gain.

Fiber – A high fiber diet will prevent elderly individuals from suffering bowel problems. Cereal foods, fruits – especially bananas – and vegetables are just some examples of food containing high fiber content. As it is with anything, sticking to a diet that's especially high in fiber is not good for the health. So make sure that your parents balance the effect of fiber to their bodies by encouraging them to drink more water than usual.

Sugar – Naturally, everything sweet is forbidden to elderly diabetic individuals. For the rest, eating a moderate amount of sugar is acceptable, more so if the person is in need of gaining weight.

Iron – As people grow older, iron deficiency becomes a more common factor. To prevent your parents from suffering from iron deficiency and consequently, anemia, make sure that they eat food high in iron like red meat, dried fruit, and green vegetables. Iron intake will also produce more benefits if it is accompanied with an increased consumption of vitamin C.

Calcium – Many advertisements nowadays emphasize the need of preventing bones from getting brittle as you get old. You do this by increasing your intake of calcium. Calcium can be found in milk and other dairy foods. Be sure to choose a milk product that's specially formulated for elderly individuals.

Zinc – Although not as popular as other minerals, zinc actually plays a significant role in an elderly individual's diet. Zinc makes wounds heal faster, something that people with diabetes would especially welcome. This mineral can be found in meat, whole meal bread, and shellfish.

Other Tips for Aging Parents to Remain Healthy

Exercise is always the partner of diet; make sure that your parents exercise regularly, even if you have to force them to do so.

If your parents are suffering from loss of appetite, let them indulge once in a while with a glass or two of alcohol as it is very good at stimulating one's desire for food. Remember however that moderation is the key to healthiness!

Moving and Your Older Relative

The Stress and Strain of Moving

Normally, moving from house to house is already a very stressful activity. It involves a great deal of inconvenience to those involved. If this is the case for people who are normally mobile, imagine what great lengths those who are immobile and or are elderly have to go through when they have to move.

Older people can go through incredible stress and depression in the move. Often, they have lived in the same home for a long time, and even if they have not, moving from completely independent living to a community can mean admitting to dependence. A change of home is stressful to anyone, but it particularly stressful for an older adult.

When you are elderly or disabled moving about is not as simple as it once was. Due to their advanced age, ailments and probable disabilities, it is harder for these people to get around, let alone move from residence to residence. If you are planning to move along with an elderly relative or parent, it would do well to remember a few pointers.

First of all there are two categories of things you must look at. You must consider the place you are moving to. And you have to make sure that the move itself is convenient or at least bearable to your elderly. It should be understood that moving from one place to another is doubly hard for those advanced in age.

Getting ready to move

The first thing you have to make sure of is that you make your elderly understand that they are moving to another place. This would relieve some of the stress that they feel due to the move. They will need the lead time to prepare themselves emotionally and physically for the transfer.

While the time needed for most people to prepare themselves for such a thing varies from person to person, and situation to situation, a notification time of about two weeks should be enough for one to be able to prepare for the move.

Your elderly will probably want to see goodbye to friends and neighbors whom they might not be able to see for a long time. They will also need to get used to the idea that their surroundings will be different in a few weeks' time.

If your elderly suffers from dementia or Alzheimer's, it still makes sense to tell them that they are moving so that somehow they still get the picture. You also want to make the place they are moving to as comfortable as possible for them. This can be done by surrounding their new environs with familiar things.

Preparing the place they are moving to

Another important part of getting an elderly ready to move is to make sure that the place they are moving to is not intimidating to them. This can be done by surrounding their rooms or their living quarters with things they are familiar with. Photo albums, pictures, and other keepsakes should do well to keep them attached to their family emotionally.

You also have to make sure that the place they are moving to has proper care ready for them. This means that it would be better if they had someone to accompany them in the new residence. Family members and friends do well for this sort of thing.

Safety precautions

You'll also have to make sure that your elderly is safe throughout the trip and in the new place they are moving to. It would do well to ready medications throughout the trip especially if it is a long one. These medications should consist of anti-nauseating pills, medications for any condition they may have, and others.

You should also make sure that during the travel they are secure and safe. Be prepared to make frequent stops and take care of their needs. Railings and hand bars should be readily accessible in case they need extra support.

And for the place they're moving to, you should make sure that the area is also elder friendly. This means that there should be railings and amenities tailor-fit for elderly people. This is to ensure they do not encounter nasty falls and spills that are common with elderly people.

Make sure you make every arrangement necessary

Before moving you should make sure that the financial aspects of the move are in place. For example, it should be clear how the bills would be paid for in the place your elderly is moving in to. Talk to the elderly and make sure they understand how things are going to work from now on.

This moving is a new experience for them, and they will be at a loss for things they do not yet understand. Let them know how you will be taking care of them, and how they are going to go about their lives, and what to expect of the place they're moving to.

If you follow these pointers, you are well on your way to making sure your elder has a comfortable experience moving to a new place. It would also do well if you were to consult with doctors and family members on the arrangements of the move

Dealing with Depression in Older People

Depression in the Elderly: Causes and Cures

Unlike what most people say, depression among the elderly is not a normal thing. It is not a normal part of aging-in fact; it is a medical condition in any age that should receive adequate treatment. Studies have shown that if depression is untreated it could lead to an increased risk of elderly suicide – more than in any other age group.

For those over 65 years of age, the signs of depression are usually ignored because they are said to be a normal part of aging. However depression is never a normal part of any age-related process-and should never be thought of as normal in any age bracket. It doesn't matter if your old or young-depression is a disease that should be treated immediately.

Definition of depression

Depression is a general feeling of being down emotionally. A person suffering from depression may feel bad about a multitude of things. Depression can strike suddenly, or can come about slowly. It can be chronic or episodic.

The best way to define depression would be to describe what it is not. Depression can then be said to be the opposite of elation, or of excitement. Depressed people are usually, but not always, grumpy, moody, lethargic, or introspective.

What causes depression?

Depression can be caused by a host of reasons. Some are emotional, and some are physical in nature. Psychological factors that cause depression include traumatic experiences a person may have experienced in the past and unresolved emotional issues.

Many of the unresolved issues a person may have had when he or she was a child may surface when the person enters advanced age. This is probably because they have more time to reflect on themselves as opposed to being busy and occupied during their younger years.

Elderly people are also prone to depression because of a fear of death, or insecurity with their now diminished physical capabilities. They may also be frustrated because of the inability to handle their memory loss.

Also, moving from one place to another can cause a great deal of stress in elderly people. The environment an elderly lives in also constitutes their emotional health. For example, if the environs they are living in are depressive, then they would naturally feel the same way.

Being elderly also means that, perhaps, many of their friends and relatives have already passed away. This can cause a great deal of stress for people to lose many of their acquaintances.

And last, but not the least, some people who face depression in their advanced age is because of the fact that depression runs in their families.

No matter what the reason, it is imperative that those looking after a people should be observant, looking for signs and symptoms of depression, and seeking treatment as soon as possible.

Here are some of the symptoms that indicate depression:

- A sudden state of being agitated.
- Anxiety that is either hard to explain or obvious
- Complaining of physical ailments that are vague or inexplicable.
- A difficulty with memory, or a lack of focus
- Lack of appetite, fluctuations in weight and health.
- Irritability and sudden emotional outbursts.
- Sleep related problems, insomnia, nightmares.

Treatment for depression

To treat depression, the first thing that must be done is to recognize that there is a problem. This is where those that care for elderly come in. They must be very observant and very quick to note changes in regular habits.

Treatment usually includes psychotherapy, counseling, medications, lifestyle modification, diet modification, and other depression related therapies. But aside from all these treatments, it is very important that there is someone to assist and guide the elderly as they go through this stage of their life. They should be given attention on and should be treated as a part of the family instead of being just a burden. This will help them feel a part of the living, and it will help reduce incidences of depression.

It is very important that people realize how dangerous depression can be for the elderly. It can cause them to get sick a lot more often than those of sound emotional health. Also, recognition and treatment of the condition early is the key to keeping good emotional health among the elderly.

Safe Driving

Creating a Driving Plan for Your Elderly: When Driving is No Longer an Option

In today's fast-paced and ever-changing world, getting from one place to another is very important. It is this increase of mobility that has helped the modern world advance to where it is now. In the United States, it is hard to imagine not having an automobile for daily chores and work.

However, as one ages or acquires some disabilities, using an automobile can be a dangerous proposition. Not being able to use an automobile seriously limits one's mobility and ability to get from one place to another. For some people, this is not even an option.

So how are those who suddenly find that driving is not an option find increased mobility and transportation? First of all, it is important to know the facts regarding the situation before making an assessment to on what to do regarding it.

Dangers of driving for the elderly

First of all, it is important to note how dangerous it is for the elderly to drive beyond the age of 65. Studies have shown that drivers over the age of 75 have the second-highest accident rate of all drivers in United States - second only to those 25 and below.

Also, those of this age bracket, when encountering accidents have double the fatality rate as opposed to any age group. This means that aside from being prone to accidents, elderly people are in greater risk of death due to these accidents. This makes taking precaution for elderly people a must for people of all ages.

However, if the elderly are stripped of the permission to drive it may cost them to feel more isolated from society in general. This could also lead to depression and a sense of uselessness. This is quite a conundrum. How are we supposed to balance the dangers of elderly driving, and the dangers of alienating them from society?

Create a driving plan

There are some ways wherein the elderly can still be given mobility and transportation while reducing the dangers of vehicular accidents due to elderly driving. This involves creating a driving plan that allows for people to assist elderly people while driving or actually driving for the elderly people.

Here are a few tips to help you create a driving plan for your older relative.

1. <u>Consider the elder's past driving record</u>. You will want to look into the history of the elder in question. Specific things to look for are traffic citations, crashes, and other vehicular mishaps the person may have experienced in the past.

Their past record may hold the key to their driving habits and their tendencies. And if you are in knowledge of their habits and tendencies, it becomes easier to predict how it will drive and how to care for these people so that they do not encounter any of the previous mishaps they have experienced.

2. <u>Look at physical or mental disabilities that may impair driving skills</u>. Take a good look at the person's medical record to find out whether he or she is fit to drive. Pay close attention to eyesight, seizures, heart conditions, and other factors that may prevent one from driving.

You may want to have a physician give his opinion on the physical sufficiency of the driver. Also, take a long hard look at the person's medication records. Look if there are any medications that may impair one's ability to comprehend or react to a traffic situation. Look for medications that cause drowsiness, decreased attention and focus, and other effects.

3. <u>Create a driving plan</u>. A driving plan means that you should schedule the traveling time among those caring for the elderly so that there is always someone who can take the person to wherever they need to go to. This could be done so that someone always accompanies the elder, or someone drives for him or her instead.

If this is not possible, then it would be good to schedule trips to places where the elderly want to go so that it is convenient to all parties involved.

In creating a driving plan for your older relative, make sure that he or she understands why this is being done for them. Also make sure that the other the not feel like he or she is a burden to the family, and that the only thing in your mind is the safety of the person in question.

Elder Safety

Preventing Falling Accidents in the Elderly

As one grows older, some of the common injuries that people are usually able to shrug off becomes startlingly grave and could cause long-term damage. For example, tripping and falling over would usually be something beneath your notice. However, as one loses mobility and physical capabilities, falls and spills become a major concern.

In the elderly, falls can be quite dangerous since as one ages, bones become more brittle. Bone density decreases dramatically after the age of 65 or even less, depending on one's diet and genetic predisposition. Since falling is now a major risk for all elderly, clearly, there should be steps undertaken to prevent injuries as a result of such.

The Facts

The sad facts show that the risk of falling increases with age. And those that do fall usually fall again within six months. As mentioned earlier, lessened bone density make each fall potentially hazardous, resulting in injuries that could be major or minor.

This is further exacerbated if the elderly do not exercise at all. A lack of exercise will result in decreased muscle strength and tone. Bone mass and density also suffer as a result of this lack of exercise. One's diet also impacts how much strength and bone density is lost in the advancing years.

However, one of the biggest factors in the increase of falling accidents of all elderly people is the fact that many homes are ill-equipped to care for elders. Most homes are an environmental hazard to elderly people. Luckily, it is not that difficult or cumbersome to rearrange your home to fit elderly people and their lifestyle.

A few tips to help the elderly cope with this type of problem in their environment

1. **Diet** - most of the elderly beyond the age of 65 show some form of osteoporosis. This is caused by many factors, one of them is diet. To help your elderly avoid injuries of this kind, it would be best to help them with their diet. They should be able to meet their needs from calcium supplements and sufficient vitamin D.

Calcium is easily available in foods such as milk, cheese, tofu, soybeans, broccoli, and calcium supplements. Vitamin D, on the other hand, is naturally formed after exposure to sunlight. However, some adults might need vitamin D supplements instead.

These are the best ways to prevent or treat osteoporosis. In addition to this, it would be best to consult with a physician or a dietitian on the proper diet for elderly people.

2. **Exercise** - This is one of the best ways to make sure that elderly people are strong enough to avoid falling or injuring themselves at home. As mentioned earlier, a lack of exercise leads to a decrease in muscle strength, and bone density.

Although people lose muscle strength as they grow older, even people of advanced age can still build muscle mass and undergo strength training. This has the effect of making the person healthier, stronger, have better balance, and have a better overall countenance.

The type of exercise they are to undergo should depend on their current abilities. It would be best to consult with a physician on a proper exercise regimen to strengthen their bodies without having to expose your elder to the injuries that usually accompany such exercise.

Good posture is also important for the elderly avoid injuries. Simply teaching them how to bend over properly, how to stand properly, and how to best handle their bodies, will go a long way in the battle against falling injuries.

3. **Elderly friendly environment** - one of the best ways to avoid having your elderly fall and injure themselves is to make sure that their environment is conducive to people with decreased mobility. Make sure there are handrails and bars around for them to hold onto while moving around. Also make sure that steps are easy to manage. If your budget allows, installing ramps instead of stars would be the best route to take.

Also make sure that the floors are not slippery. It would be better if there were some rubber padding to help them keep their traction. Also supply them with good shoes so they don't slip as easy as before.

Understanding Confusion

Understanding Confusion among Your Elderly Parents

Elderly individuals do not get "senile" due to old age. Medically, this is called sudden or dreaded arrival of confusion or delirium. The incidence of delirium or confusion in hospitalized elderly patients from 80 years old and above varies from 35-50 percent. Delirium is generally viewed as puzzlement to space and time.

Acute confusion or delirium is in fact temporary, have an unexpected onset and can be identifiable by numerous inappropriate behaviors.

The behaviors related with delirium can include sleep disturbances, inattentiveness, hallucinations, disjointed speech and other obvious changes in the central functioning of the nervous system.

Confusion and dementia

A confused elder does not essentially have dementia. Problems in clearly communicating as well as memory loss often are symptoms of dementia however it is not proper to presume that somebody who is forgetful or confused has dementia.

Confusion is generally just one among the many signs of dementia. An elderly with dementia most certainly will be confused sometimes, but not all the time.

There are many reasons why specifically the elderly may seem confused. In fact, nearly 20 percent of elders go through depression that may cause difficulty thinking and remembering.

Medications also can cause thinking problems. Dietary deficiencies, Drug mixes, excess consumption of alcohol as well as other factors may bring about signs similar that to dementia.

Causes

Delirium is usually brought about by depression, infection specifically urinary tract and respiratory infections and nutritional imbalances; decrease in blood pressure, dehydration, sensory overload or deprivation and drugs also can cause delirium.

Studies have established that approximately one in every three elderly persons undergoes some type of depression in their life.

Social isolation. Not having or lacking in social interaction as well as prolonged loneliness can bring on confusion or bizarre behavior. There is a recently identified pathology called, "isolation dementia" which has no brain attributes, but has mostly psychological attributes. Studies are ongoing in this area as gerontologists believe this could actually be a very common form of dementia.

Infections. Fever due to infections alone may be responsible for bringing about confusion. Generally, confusion resulting from infection or fever is referred to as delirium. An elderly patient in a delirious state will appear sick and drowsy, while a frantic patient is "ready to go" and wide awake. As elderly persons age, note that their brains cannot tolerate fever well.

Stroke. Note that the single most notable sign that an elderly person is undergoing a stroke can be confusion, typically identified by concurrent weakness or neurological abnormality.

Diabetes. When the elderly person's blood sugar decreases to very low levels or in hypoglycemia they become confused.

Heart failure. In fact, as the heart condition worsens, the need of the elderly for oxygen also increases. Confusion happens when somebody requiring supplemental oxygen generally is not obtaining adequate amounts.

Drugs. A lot of drugs that are prescribed by physicians can lead or cause confusion. These medications are narcotics which are used primarily for pain, antipsychotics antidepressants used for psychiatric disorders treatment and also sleeping pills.

These medicines are often used at their recommended dosage for adults; however elderly individuals can acquire side effects even at recommended levels.

Here are some medications that may cause confusion:

- Mellaril-thioridazine
- Endep, Elavil-amitriptyline
- Elavil, Triavil, Etrafon, Endep-tricyclic antidepressants
- Sal Tropine-Limbitrol atropine
- Slo-Phyllin, Slo-Bid, Aerolate, Accurbron- theophylline
- Sleep-Eze, Benadryl, Unisom-diphenhydramine
- Actifed, Contac, Triaminic, Allerest, Tavist-containing pseudoephedrine HCL and phenylprop HCL
- Tagamet-cimetidine
- Demerol-merperidine
- Naproxen, Naprosyn- anti-inflammatory nonsterodoidal drugs
- Triazolam, Halcion- halcion
- Dalmane, Ativan, Librium, Diazepam, Restoril, Serax, Lorazepam, Valium, Tranxene, Xanax-benzidiazepines cardiovascular drugs
- Procardia, Adalat-nifedipine
- Qinaglute-quinidine
- Inderal, Betachron, Cardizem, Propranolol, Adalat, Cardene, Vasotec, Vascor, Lanoxin, Lopressor-beta blockers

Changes in the elderly person's environment. Relocating from the elderly person's residence to a hospital or nursing home, from a nursing community to another may result in an episode of confusion.

The relocation can be considered by elderly people as a "life-threatening" event because their social group is destroyed or they struggle to adapt to their strange and new surroundings.

Note that there are various reasons for elderly persons to be confused. Some types of confusion are without difficulty curable, others are treatable while others are terminal. Therefore, there must be a careful search and assessment for a reason as soon as confusion is noticed.

Know the Professionals

Geriatric Care Manager

Nearly 6 million American seniors need help with very basic activities such as dressing, "getting out of bed", cooking, cleaning as well as handling finances. As a natural consequence, about 4 million Americans are caring for their aging parent.

Families are now turning to a dedicated team of professionals to assist or help them care for their elderly relatives.

"Geriatric care managers" or GCM, unknown 21 years ago, now are rapidly emerging into a significant part of the system for elderly care.

Elder care involves obtaining the best custodial and medical care at the most cost-effective and dignified way for your parents or any loved one. Successful eldercare involves knowledge, planning, patience and action.

A professional "Geriatric Care Manager" is a human and health services professional, like a nurse, gerontologist, psychologist or social worker having a specialized education that focus on subjects related to elderly care. These professionals underwent extensive training as well as ample experience working with families and elderly persons who require support with elderly care giving concerns.

A GCM will evaluate your family's situation, establish solutions then with your participation, devise a plan for make the most of your love one's well-being and independence. Simply put, "geriatric care management" requires in-depth assessment, making an elderly care plan, organizing elderly services and monitoring care.

While you are not obliged to put into practice any portion of the CGM's suggested elderly care plan, "geriatric care managers" suggest possible alternatives that you may not have taken into account, because of their familiarity and experience with community sources.

Benefits of hiring a "geriatric care manager"

You may hire a "geriatric care manager" for just one, specific task like helping you discover a daily elder caregiver or to manage or direct the whole elderly care giving process. "Geriatric care managers" help elderly persons and their families who are:

- New to elderly care or not comfortable with decision-making regarding elder care

- Have difficulty with some aspect of elderly care

- Faced with unexpected decision or huge change like a health emergency or relocation

- Dealing with complex situation like cognitive, psychiatric, legal, and social or health issue.

Choosing a geriatric care manager

It is very important to note that the area of "geriatric care management" is somewhat unregulated and a lot of individuals recognize themselves as "geriatric care managers" even without any specialized training, care advisors or care coordinators.

Here are suggestions in choosing your "geriatric care manager":

- Ask about the candidates' education, training as well as background or experience in elderly care management. Ask whether or not they are a member of the "National Association of Professional Geriatric Care Managers".

- Ask the candidate what is her usual response time when returning calls from their clients.

- Ask how "after-hours" emergencies are dealt with? Do they have "back-up systems" for covering days off or vacation? If there is, have them describe what it is.

- Find out the GCM's scope of practice. Note that several GCMs specialize in care consultation and assessments however normally do not monitor the elderly regularly.

There are GCMs that offer money management, psychotherapy, and home care. Likewise, they can function as conservators who are court-appointed to manage or direct the financial or personal affairs the elderly person who is unable to supervise or manage his own affairs.

Examine the GCM's reputation and track record. Ask for names of past clients that you can contact and letters of recommendation.

Keep in mind, whereas GCM's have no "licensing requirements", there are in fact certification programs. Make certain you request each candidate that you will interview for a certification.

Cost of hiring "geriatric care manager"

Fees of private "geriatric care managers" can vary from 75-200 dollars per hour which depends on what types of services you require.

While this seems costly, note that a "geriatric care manager" will ultimately save you much money by evaluating your exact needs as well as helping you select the particular services that best can serve you.

Even though fees of "geriatric care management" are not "covered" by Medicaid or Medicare, some insurance companies, employers, "financial service providers" and health plans are now beginning to cover or subsidize these forms of services for their clients and members.

Hiring somebody to help you look after or care for your elderly parent is indeed a very serious, however often an essential, thing to decide on. You need to make sure that the GCM will be your ears and eyes and more importantly, bring unto your elderly parent's care abundance of resources, compassion and understanding.

The Elder Law Attorney

What is Elder Law?

In recent years, a new area of law has emerged, that many are calling "Elder Law". Rather than being defined by technical legal distinctions, elder law is defined by the client to be served. In other words, a lawyer who practices elder law may handle a range of issues but has a specific type of clients--seniors.

Attorneys who practice in the area of elder law focus on the legal needs of the elderly, and work with a variety of legal tools and techniques to meet the goals and objectives of the older client.

Under this holistic approach, elder law attorneys handle general estate planning issues and counsel clients about planning for incapacity with alternative decision making documents. I also assist my clients in planning for possible long-term care needs, including nursing home care. Locating the appropriate type of care, coordinating private and public resources to finance the cost of care, and working to ensure the client's right to quality care are all part of the elder law practice.

Elder law has become an important area of law. One in two Americans will suffer a disability during their lifetime, requiring the appointment of someone to manage their financial affairs and make health care decisions. Not only will half of all Americans someday require the appointment of a decision-maker, but 40 percent of Americans over the age of 60 will face admission into an assisted living facility or nursing home. Proactive planning can make this situation more manageable and less costly, as well as help preserve autonomy and privacy. Lack of planning, on the other hand, can result in unnecessary court intervention, increased costs and negative tax consequences, as well as greater loss of autonomy and reduced privacy.

Why and When You May Need an Elder Law Attorney

Elder Law Attorneys have been specially trained to set up effective plans to deal with disability before it strikes and to help soften the blow when it comes. Elder Law attorneys are able to offer insight and services not found in traditional law firms. While Estate lawyers focus on death-time planning, such as distributing assets to heirs through a will or living trust, and tax lawyers focus on avoiding the estate tax with a bypass trust or other tools. Elder law attorneys, on the other hand, address not only these needs but also needs before death, preparing for periods of serious illness or incapacity. While a portion of my practice is traditional estate planning, a growing percentage of the clients I see each week come to me with elder law issues.

Elder law recognizes that people are living longer with chronic illnesses and will face periods of either short-term or long-term incapacity. These chronic illnesses cause impairments that result in long-term care expenses and loss of independence. Elder law attorneys help senior citizens preserve their independence, avoid impoverishment and implement their desire to pass their estate to loved ones.

Without proper planning, incapacity can very often mean guardianship. When a court guardianship is imposed, the individual judged to be incapacitated loses autonomy. The procedure can be expensive, frustrating and time-consuming. Elder law attorneys provide assistance to avoid guardianships and are able to consult with you to create an effective and comprehensive incapacity plan. It may include drafting new wills with special provisions, powers of attorney, health care powers of attorney, or consulting on how to pay for the devastating cost of nursing homes, through Medicaid and Veterans benefits planning.

Elder Law is Complicated

Unfortunately, Elder Law is complicated because it encompasses a variety of areas of law. It is unrealistic to think one elder law attorney can have expertise in each. The Elder law attorney, however, should have familiarity with these areas, and be able to bring experts in when needed in other areas.

Some of these include:

- Preservation/transfer of assets seeking to avoid spousal impoverishment when a spouse enters a nursing home
- Medicaid
- Medicare claims and appeals
- Social security and disability claims and appeals
- Supplemental and long term health insurance issues.
- Disability planning, including use of durable powers of attorney, living trusts, "living wills," for financial management and health care decisions, and other means of delegating management and decision-making to another in case of incompetency or incapacity.
- Conservatorships and guardianships

- Estate planning, including planning for the management of one's estate during life and its disposition on death through the use of trusts, wills and other planning documents
- Probate
- Administration and management of trusts and estates
- Long-term care placements in nursing home and life care communities
- Nursing home issues including questions of patients' rights and nursing home quality
- Elder abuse and fraud recovery cases
- Housing issues, including discrimination and home equity conversions
- Age discrimination in employment
- Retirement, including public and private retirement benefits, survivor benefits and pension benefits
- Health law
- Mental health law

Most elder law attorneys do not specialize in every one of these areas. So when an attorney says he/she practices Elder Law, find out which of these matters he/she handles. You will want to hire the attorney who regularly handles matters in the area of concern in your particular case and who will know enough about the other fields to question whether the action being taken might be affected by laws in any of the other areas of law on the list. For example, if you are going to rewrite your will and your spouse is ill, the estate planner needs to know enough about Medicaid to know whether it is an issue with regard to your spouse's inheritance.

Attorneys who primarily work with the elderly bring more to their practice than an expertise in the appropriate area of law. They bring to their practice a knowledge of the elderly that allows them and their staff to ignore the myths relating to aging and the competence of the elderly. At the same time, they will take into account and empathize with some of the true physical and mental difficulties that often accompany the aging process. Their understanding of the afflictions of the aged allows them to determine more easily the difference between the physical versus the mental disability of a client. They are more aware of real life problems, health and otherwise, that tend to crop up as persons age. They are tied into a formal or informal system of social workers, psychologists and other elder care professionals who may be of assistance to you. All of these things will hopefully make you more comfortable when dealing with them and ease your way as you try to resolve your legal problem.

Finding an Elder Law Attorney

Your first question may be: How do I find an elder law attorney? Before making the effort, step back a moment and try to determine whether you actually have a legal problem in which an attorney needs to be involved. If you are not sure, ask your clergy, your social worker, your financial advisor, or a trusted friend to help you decide whether this is a legal issue rather than a medical or a social services issue. Legal expertise is expensive and it serves you well to know that you actually need legal assistance before seeking an attorney.

There are many places to find an attorney in your city or state who specializes in problems of the elderly. Check with local agencies to obtain good quality local referrals. Some of the agencies you may want to call include:

- The National Academy of Elder Law Attorneys
- Elderlawanswers.com
- Answersforelders.com

- Alzheimer's Association
- American Association of Retired Persons
- Area Agency (or Council) on Aging
- Children of Aging Parents
- Health Insurance Association of America
- National Citizen's Coalition of Nursing Home Reform
- Older Women's League
- Social Security Office
- State Civil Liberties Union
- State Insurance Commissioner
- State or Local Bar Association
- Support Groups for specific diseases
- Hospital or Nursing Home Social Service Department

Most of the above agencies can be found in the yellow pages under the heading "Associations."

If you know any attorneys ask them for a referral to an elder law attorney. An attorney is in a good position to know who handles such issues and whether that person is a good attorney. Such persons are often the best and safest sources of referrals.

Ask Questions First
Ask lots of questions before selecting and elder law attorney. You don't want to end up in the office of an attorney who can't help you. Start with the initial phone call. It is not unusual to speak only to a secretary, receptionist or office manager during an initial call or before actually meeting with the attorney. If so, ask this person your questions.

- How long has the attorney been in practice?
- Does his/her practice emphasize a particular area of law?
- How long has he/she been in this field?

- What percentage of his/her practice is devoted to elder law?
- Is there a fee for the first consultation and if so, how much is it?
- Given the nature of your problem, what information should you bring with you to the initial consultation?

The answers to your questions will assist you in determining whether that particular attorney has those qualifications important to you for a successful attorney/client relationship. If you have a specific legal issue that requires immediate attention, be sure to inform the office of this during the initial telephone conversation.

Once You Have Found an Elder Law Attorney
When you have found an appropriate attorney, make an appointment to see him/her. During the initial consultation, you will be asked to give the attorney an overview of the reason you are seeking assistance, so be sure to organize and bring all the information pertinent too your situation.

After you have explained your situation, ask:

- What will it take to resolve it?
- Are there any alternative courses of action?
- What are the advantages and disadvantages of each possibility?
- How many attorneys are in the office?
- Who will handle your case?
- Has that attorney handled matters of this kind in the past?
- If a trial may be involved, does he/she do trial work? If not, who does the trial work? If so, how many trials has he/she handled?
- Is that attorney a member of the local bar association, its health advocacy committee, or trust and estates committee?
- Is that attorney a member of the National Academy of Elder Law Attorneys?

- How are fees computed?
- What is his/her estimate of the cost to resolve your problem and how long will it take?

Discussing Fees

There are many different ways of charging fees and each attorney will choose to work differently. Be aware of how your attorney charges. You will also want to know how often he/she bills. Some attorneys bill weekly, some bill monthly, some bill upon completion of work. Ask about these matters at the initial conference, so there will be no surprises! If you don't understand, ask again. If you need clarification, say so. It is very important that you feel comfortable in this area.

Some attorneys charge by the hour with different hourly rates for work performed by attorneys, paralegals and secretaries. If this is the case, find out what the rates are. Other attorneys charge a flat fee for all or part of the services. This is not unusual, for example, if you are having documents prepared. Your attorney might use a combination of these billing methods.

In addition to fees, most attorneys will charge you out-of-pocket expenses. Out-of-pocket expenses typically include charges for copies, postage, messenger fees, court fees, disposition fees, long distance telephone calls and other such costs. Find out if there will be any other incidental costs.

The attorney may ask for a retainer. This is money paid before the attorney starts working on your case. It is usually placed in a trust account and each time the attorney bills you, he/she pays himself or herself out of that account. Expenses may be paid directly from the trust account. The size of the retainer may range from a small percentage of the estimated cost to the full amount.

Get It in Writing
Once you decide to hire the attorney, ask that your arrangement be put in writing. The writing can be a letter or a formal contract. It should spell out what services the attorney will perform for you and what the fee and expense arrangement will be. REMEMBER-- even if your agreement remains oral and is not put into writing, you have made a contract and are responsible for all charges for work done by the attorney and his/her staff.

Make It a Good Experience
A positive and open relationship between attorney and client benefits everyone. The key to getting it is communication. The communication starts with asking the kinds of questions contained in this document. Use the answers to the questions as a guide not only to the attorney's qualification, but also as a way of determining whether you can comfortably work with this person. If your concerns are given short shrift, if you don't like the answers to these questions, if you don't like the attorney's reaction to being asked all those questions, or if you simply do not feel relaxed with this particular person, DO NOT HIRE THAT PERSON. Only if you are satisfied with the attorney you have hired from the very start will you trust him or her to do the best job for you. Only if you have established a relationship of open communication will you be able to resolve any difficulties which may arise between the two of you. If you take the time to make sure that you are happy right at the beginning you can make this a productive experience for both you and the attorney. You will thank yourself, and your attorney will thank you.

The Gerontologist

A gerontologist is anyone who works with the elderly in one way or another, but is quickly becoming a separate profession. Many social workers are becoming "Social Gerontologists" and many universities now offer degrees in gerontology.

The field of gerontology is multidisciplinary. That means that people from many different educational backgrounds (doctors, nurses, teachers and sociologists) work as gerontologists.

Since we all age, the study of gerontology is in everyone's best interest, not just those who are seniors right now. Gerontology researchers actually study the aging process. They study how we change mentally and physically as we get older.

Some gerontologists are doctors who specialize in working with the elderly.

Teachers can also be gerontologists. They may teach the subject at a university or college level, and write about the issues of aging.

A gerontologist can be an administrator in a nursing home, an assisted living community or a senior citizens' center. They try to provide the most comfortable environment for the elderly.

Since gerontology includes many different professions, people in this field are hired in various positions and settings.

The Geriatric Physician

If you are getting older and having more health problems you may want to consider seeing a doctor who specializes in geriatric medicine.

A geriatrician is a physician who has completed a residency in either Internal Medicine or Family Medicine with an additional one or two year fellowship training in the medical, social, and psychological issues that concern older adults. This specialty is increasing in importance as the population ages and that aging population lives longer. People over the age of 85 are the fast growing segment of the population. It is no longer a rarity for people to live to be one hundred.

A geriatrician is a doctor who specializes in care for people 65 and older. Just as a pediatrician tends to the needs of a child, a geriatrician cares for the special needs of changing seniors. Geriatrician's approach each patient's needs individually, and possess the knowledge and expertise needed to accommodate seniors. They are typically board certified in Internal Medicine and have additional training in areas pertaining to elder care. They can better address issues such as memory loss, arthritis, osteoporosis, mobility and Alzheimer's disease. Clearly, geriatrics includes more than treating physical problems; it means recognizing how health conditions affect seniors socially and emotionally, and vice versa.

Seniors often associate age with disease. Yet, aging does not cause diseases. While many seniors believe that the reason they are not feeling well is because they are getting older, this is not always the case. The problems they are experiencing may be related to an illness or injury not at all caused by age. This is why it is important to seek the helpful knowledge of a geriatrician.

This type of physician practice far exceeds simply diagnosing a physical problem and treating it. Geriatricians collect information about patients' lifestyles, community, family, and their entire medical history.

The most appropriate term for a physician who specializes in the care of older adults is geriatrician, not gerontologist. A gerontologist is generally a non-physician, though physicians who focus on aging research can also be considered gerontologists.

Questions People Ask About Geriatricians

What is a Geriatrician?
A Geriatrician is a professional who studies the aging process. A Geriatrician also studies how to prevent diseases. One of the biggest issues for a Geriatrician is to prevent and treat dementia.

Who should visit a Geriatrician?
Older people who have an increase in health problems should seek help from a Geriatrician. Although the field is in an evolving state, it is

likely that more people will seek out geriatricians as primary care physicians as they get older. It only makes sense that someone trained in the particular issues of becoming older, would be an excellent person to serve as a primary care physician.

Where does a Geriatrician work?
A Geriatrician can work in an elderly facility, a hospital, a clinic, or in private practice.

What is the difference between a Geriatrician and a Gerontologist?
A Geriatrician treats and prevents the ill-effects of aging while a Gerontologist simply studies the aging process itself, or works in a non-medical field associated with elder people.

Take Care of the Caregiver: Preventing and Identifying Caregiver Stress

Caring for an elderly individual takes much effort, time, and work. Plus, almost all caregivers squeeze in care giving with parenting and putting their personal needs aside during the process. New research indicates that there is a direct and negative toll on primary caregivers, including the need for care themselves at an earlier age.

Caregivers report often that normally it is very hard to monitor their personal health specifically nutrition, doctor visits and exercise, ending up feeling anxious, angry, sad and isolated.

Studies indicate that elderly care giving "takes a toll" on emotional and physical health. Note that caregivers are likely to experience depression compared to their non-care giving peers.

Furthermore, studies revealed that elderly caregivers also are more prone to experiencing health problems such as heart disease and diabetes compared to non-caregivers.

Caregivers for those suffering from Alzheimer's disease or other types of dementia in elderly are especially vulnerable to suffer exhaustion. Research indicates that almost all dementia caregivers go through stress and depression.

Causes of caregiver stress

Role confusion. Many individuals are confused if pushed into a care giving role, as it is hard for some individuals to detach her function as an elderly caregiver from the function of being a lover, spouse, friend, mother, child, etc.

Unrealistic expectations. A lot of elderly caregivers expect that their involvement will have an encouraging effect on their patient's happiness and health. However, this can be unrealistic because patients that are suffering Alzheimer's or Parkinson's are in fact are progressive illnesses.

Lacking control. Caregivers usually become upset when they lack resources, skills and money to successfully manage, organize and their patient's care.

Unreasonable demands. There are caregivers that place

unreasonable weight upon themselves, partly because they view caring for their patient is their sole responsibility.

Preventing caregiver stress

There are a number of things that you can do to take care of yourself if you are a caregiver. Here are a few ideas.

- First, find somebody that you can trust like your co-worker, neighbor or friend and talk to them about your frustrations.

- Only set realistic objectives and acknowledge that you need help caring with your parent and ask for help to other family members for assistance with certain tasks.

- Be sensible about your elderly parent's illness especially if they are suffering from a progressive ailment like Alzheimer's or Parkinson's.

- Make sure that you also care for yourself. Never be too busy taking care of your elderly parents that you forget to set some time aside for yourself even just for an hour. Caring for yourself is an absolute requirement for caregivers.

- Consult a professional such as a social worker, a clergy member or a therapist as they are well trained to advice and support individuals who deal with some type of emotional and physical issues.

- Hire the help of elderly "respite care" services. They provide a break temporarily for caregivers, ranging from several hours of "in-home" care to just a brief stay in an assisted living home facility or nursing home.

- Know what your limits are then do a "reality check" of your situation. Identify and accept your possibility for caregiver stress.

- Educate yourself. In fact, the more that you are familiar with your elderly parent's illness, the more successful you can be in taking care of your elder.

- Develop new means for coping. Keep in mind to always lighten up as well as accentuate at all times the positive. You can use humor to help you deal with your everyday stress.

- Stay healthy by means of having regular exercise, eating right and getting enough sleep.

- Keep in mind that stress is not the same as having flu or experiencing a cold. In fact, you will not notice it always while you are undergoing it. However, by recognize or admitting the reality or fact that care giving is often times filled with anxiety and stress, and accepting the possibility for stress, you as a caregiver will be forewarned as well as guarded against this incapacitating condition.

Aside from stress, a lot of caregivers declare that their role when caring for their elderly parents has had a lot of positive outcome on their life. For instance, many state that taking care of their loved one has brought about a "sense of purpose" in them. Their care giving role had made them feel very capable, useful and that indeed, they are creating a big difference their loved one's life.

Conclusion

It is estimated that children will spend more time caring for their parents than they did caring for their own children. With the challenges of longevity, health issues, caregiving and housing issues and legal issues, the job is complex. Fortunately, there are more professionals available to help take the load from you as the responsible child. Make use of these professionals.

Caring for others is by far the most difficult job in the world. But when equipped with the proper support, information and guidance, this daunting job can be much lighter. If you are in a position where you are caring for an older relative, I hope that this book has provided enough guidance for you to feel you job has been lightened, if just a bit.

Don't be afraid to seek help, whether it is in the form of family support, financial support or legal support. And while caregiving is difficult, it is not without its rewards. Keeping perspective of these facts, I hope, will give you the opportunity to make your burden just a bit lighter.

As a person who not only serves clients professionally in the elder care arena, but who has also taken care of his parents, I understand much of what you, as a child, is going through. My professional life has been dedicated to helping to ease the load. Many professionals do so also. I wish you the best in your pursuits, and hope that this book has been helpful.

www.ingramcontent.com/pod-product-compliance
Lightning Source LLC
Chambersburg PA
CBHW022006170526
45157CB00003B/1167